The Key

Is

To Be

(A Practical Primer for Pastors)

The Key Is To Be

(A Practical Primer for Pastors)

Dr. Michael P. Haynes

ISBN 978-0-557-33434-6

**Dedicated to the pastors of the
Greene County Baptist Association.
These men are my brothers,
friends and heroes.**

When I mention the name of a pastor
I will place the name of the church where
they serve as pastor, co-pastor or associate
pastor in parenthesis.

CONTENTS

Acknowledgements .... *ix*

Introduction .... *xi*

Chapter One: *The Key Is To Be* *1*

Chapter Two: *Your Church's Top Priority* *15*

Chapter Three: *Cherish Your Family* *27*

Chapter Four: *Don't Waste Pain* *41*

Chapter Five: *Balance* *55*

Chapter Six: *What's A Pastor To Do?*

(Don't Resign – Until It's Time) *65*

Chapter Seven: *Leadership* *87*

Conclusion *97*

Sources *99*

ACKNOWLEDGEMENTS

I am blessed.

I enjoy the finest wife a man can have. Robbi is my best friend, strongest encourager and the joy of my life. Life is a blast with my Robbi.

I have the greatest kids and kids-in-law anywhere. I am so proud of Josh and Heather Haynes and Heidi and Damon Hargraves. Their lives and service are a constant inspiration to me.

Robbi and the kids gave invaluable assistance in writing this book. They gave me permission to share personal stories and they read and critiqued the manuscript.

I am honored to have served as pastor of three wonderful churches: Blue Summit Baptist Church, Kansas City, MO (1977-1984); Antioch Southern Baptist Church, Harrisonville, MO (1984-1988); First Baptist Church, North Kansas City, MO (1988-1998).

It is a privilege beyond words to serve as the Director of the Greene County Baptist Association, Springfield, MO (1988-present). I thank my Association for the privilege of a Sabbatical in early 2009. This gave me time, freedom and focus to write this book.

I thank my Assistant, Terry Wright. She is both a teammate in ministry and a dear friend. Her encouragement and manuscript work have been invaluable to me.

My Associational staff is the best.

I thank the pastors who reviewed the manuscript and gave insightful and necessary feedback: Hosea Bilyeu (Ridgecrest); Nolan Carrier (South Gate); Mike Graves (NorthBridge); Ty Harmon (Galloway); Boone Middleton (Golden Avenue); John Marshall (Second Baptist); Morton Rose (former Interim at First Baptist Church, Springfield); Doug Shivers (Boulevard).

I also thank Hosea, Nolan, John, Doug and Gary Merkel (Harmony) for allowing me to tell their stories.

INTRODUCTION

I love pastors. Pastors have a divine and difficult calling. Pastors love their work, but they carry a heavy burden only other pastors can understand.

My calling is to bless, encourage and train pastors. This is not only my calling—it is my privilege. I am awe-struck that God invited me to share in the ministry of helping pastors. This book is an outgrowth of my calling.

One section of my **Personal Mission Statement** says, "I will *leverage* my life to make the greatest impact for Jesus." This book is one way I hope to fulfill that mission.

This is not a skill book which discusses ministry performance (preaching, administration, etc.). It is written to help pastors *be* the best persons they can *be*. Here you find the basics—*first things*. If pastors don't get these things right, skill level or performance won't matter.

The principles outlined in the book are applicable for everyone. However, the book is especially written for practicing pastors.

Chapter One

THE KEY IS TO BE

I was a young pastor and I was in trouble. I had enjoyed several successful years as a pastor when the wheels came off. It was a time when church attendance and offerings were declining. Baptisms and additions were few and far between. My preaching was weak, my vision for the church was fuzzy and my leadership inadequate. During this particular time, church leaders wondered if they made a mistake by calling me as their pastor. I didn't blame them. It seemed like everything I tried went sour. I went so far as to question my call to ministry, my competence as a pastor and my ability to succeed in any endeavor in life. I wondered: How do I measure my worth as a man and as a pastor? How do I determine if I am successful? How will I know if my life and ministry are pleasing to God?

Society says we are what we do. Our lives and success are measured by our job, our salary, our education or some other external factor. Many pastors (if not most) measure their success by their pastoral and church performance. They feel successful if Sunday attendance is good or they feel depressed if attendance is down. They feel like a winner if certain people compliment their sermon. They feel like a loser if they don't get the compliments. They feel like God is smiling on them if the church adds members or they wonder what they've done to disappoint God if the church doesn't have anyone join.

It was during this time of pain the Lord spoke to me very clearly regarding the measure of a successful life. Through my struggles, God taught me that a successful life is not about *doing*, but about *being*. Society says that we *are* what we *do*. God says the *person we are* is eternally more important than the *things we do*. In fact, who we *are* determines what we *do*. This has nothing to do with a particular job or task or even the church we serve, but everything to do with our life and God's mission for our life. Nearly everything we *do* is incidental and temporal. Who we *are* is essential and eternal. In Genesis we read, "*The Lord God formed the man...and the man became a living being.*" God made us *living beings* not *living doings*.

How do you measure your success as a person and a pastor? Does your success have to do with how big a church you pastor, how many staff you lead, how big your church's offerings are and how often you are invited to preach at an outside engagement? Do you believe your success is determined by denominational recognition, pleasing certain church leaders and completing certain pastoral duties? Those are all external factors and reveal a *doing* focus in life and ministry.

On the other hand, if your focus is primarily on *being*, you will be motivated by internal factors. Things such as knowing and using the unique gifts God has given you. Growing in character so you can be the healthiest and most joyful person you can be. You will work to develop strong personal relationships with those who are most important to you. And primarily, you will build the best relationship with the Lord you can possibly build. In other words, are you motivated by an internal compass that is rooted in *being* or are you driven by external factors that shift with the culture, environment and passing time?

Being and Doing

What do I mean when I talk about *being* and *doing*? I am using the word *doing* to mean the act or activity of doing something. It has to do with performing a task or job. For a pastor, *doing* is carrying out your assigned ministry activities. It could be preaching, visiting, leading meetings, writing a newsletter article or a myriad of tasks a pastor has to regularly perform. On the other hand, *being* refers to the nature and character of a person. It involves knowing yourself, growing in who you *are* as a person and *being* the best *you* that you can be. It involves internalizing and developing the beatitudes. In Matthew chapter 5 Jesus gives us the beginning point of *being*. In the "be"attitudes he talks about being poor in spirit, mourning, developing meekness, hungering and thirsting after righteousness, showing mercy and being peacemakers.

Being has to do with developing integrity. Integrity is when your outside (behavior) matches your inside (character). People who have integrity are people whose lives are integrated (unified). They are not two-faced. They are whole. In other words, not trying to be someone they are not. *Being* is living your true character in every decision you make and every relationship you have. *Being* is focusing on your internal self and then working, struggling, praying and seeking to be the exact person God created, saved, gifted and called you to be. Nothing more and nothing less. Just simply the best *you* that you can be. There is no task in the world more challenging and exhilarating than that.

Kurt Warner and Me

Becoming who God made us to *be* is a life-long endeavor. If we *become* who God made us to *be* then effective *doing* will naturally follow. If we *become* the best we can *be*, we will do extraordinary things with our lives. We will achieve heights we never imagined possible. But, if we try to do things that are not who we are, we will fail miserably.

I am writing this in the winter of 2009. Kurt Warner and the Arizona Cardinals have recently lost Super Bowl XLIII to the Pittsburg Steelers. I was pulling for the Cardinals. When I was a boy I dreamed of playing quarterback in the NFL (actually, I still dream that occasionally!). Truth is, as much I might dream it, I don't have one Kurt Warner pass in me. However hard I tried I could never throw one pass as fast, far and accurate as Warner throws them every down. It is simply not in me. It is not who I am. On the other hand, I doubt Warner has even one of my sermons in him. I bet he can't organize as successful a leadership seminar as I can or encourage a hurting pastor as well as me. That is not who he is. Effective living is about *being* who we are.

My Dad is 6 ft. 3 in. tall and was an outstanding high school and college basketball player. As a teenager, my goal was to be taller than my Dad. I stopped growing in the eighth grade at 5 ft. 9 in. One time I was visiting with a pastor friend when he suddenly interjected, "Mike, your deep voice is to a preacher what a 6 ft. 10 in. body would be to a basketball player." I chuckled to myself as tears sprang to my eyes. I remembered my teenage goal. I then thought, "Lord, You made me exactly like You want me so that I will accomplish exactly what You want me to do. Thank you."

Our Focus

Where is our focus? Are we focused more on *doing* or *being*? At times I think I'm learning how to focus more on *being* and then something will happen and I realize I've hardly grown at all in this challenge. One way we can check our focus is by examining how we think about ourselves and how we introduce ourselves to others. When we think about ourselves do we primarily think about who we *are* or what we *do*? In other words, do we want to be known for the *person we are* or by the *things we do*? For example, when I meet someone for the first time do I say, "Hi, I'm Mike and I'm the Director of the Greene County Baptist Association." Or, do I say, "Hi, I'm Mike and I'm a child of God's and Molly and Henry's granddaddy." Sounds silly, but think about it. If our focus is on *doing*, we want to be known by *what we do*. We want to be known by our job or work title. But, if we want to be known by *who we are*, we will talk about the *being* part of our lives. One way or another we clearly announce the focus of our lives. We let others know what our lives are about.

We have an example of this in scripture. How did God introduce Himself to Moses? As Moses stood before the burning bush, did God announce Himself by what He did or who He was? *"Moses said to God, 'Suppose I go to the Israelites and say to them, 'The God of your fathers has sent me to you,' and they ask me, 'What is his name?' Then what shall I tell them?' God said to Moses, 'I AM WHO I AM. This is what you are to say to the Israelites: 'I AM has sent me to you'."* God could have announced Himself to Moses by saying, "Tell the Israelites that the God of creation, provision and miracles has sent you." But He didn't. He introduced Himself out of *who He is* and not *what He does.*

Our Culture's Focus

We must be diligent if we are to move from a focus on *doing* to a focus on *being*. Our culture is focused almost exclusively on *doing* and it tries to mold us in its image. Think about it. Whether we are talking about business, government, education or church the conversation is on *doing* (performance). Our conversations start with: How are you doing? How is your business succeeding? What grade did you make in your class? How many did you have in Sunday School?

What if we started conversations with *being* questions? Questions like: Tell me what you've done lately for *fun*? What have you *learned* recently in school? Are employer/employee *relationships* healthy and growing at your work place? Tell me how you and your church leaders are experiencing and enjoying the presence of God?

If our focus is primarily on *doing*, then over time our performance will struggle (fail) and we will suffer. When our *doing* doesn't measure up we will experience frustration, insecurities, fear, depression and finally burn-out. The constant comparison-to-others outlook of a *doing* focus will invariably drag us down. Paul instructed the Corinthians to be careful that, *"We do not dare to classify or compare ourselves with some who commend themselves. When they measure themselves by themselves and compare themselves with themselves, they are not wise."*

The great basketball player Bill Russell got it. After retiring from basketball, Bill Russell and Wilt Chamberlain remained good friends. One time Wilt confessed to Bill that he was unhappy and unfulfilled without basketball. Bill said, "Wilt, basketball was what we did—it is not who we are."

That raises a penetrating question. If your church went away, would your life go away? I can think of several pastors who lost their church (some of their choosing and others not), and then struggled with their identity. Who are you if you don't have a church to pastor? What's left of you?

Mary and Martha are excellent examples of this tension. In Luke we read where Mary sat down at the Lord's feet while, *"Martha was distracted by all the preparation."* Martha complained to Jesus that Mary wasn't doing her fair share of the work. Jesus answered, *"Martha, Martha, you are worried and upset about many things…Mary has chosen what is better."* I remember countless times when I was busy *doing* vital stuff in the church that I was sure took priority over everything else only to look back now and realize I was missing *"what is better."*

Let me make something clear. *Doing* is important. We must do things if we are to graduate from school, compete in sports, find a job, purchase and take care of a home, raise a family and pastor a church. *The issue is focus.* Is our focus on *doing*, which makes us a victim of culture's expectations and others opinions? Or, is our focus on *being,* which leads to the knowledge of God's design for our lives and results in fruit that is in keeping with God's plan?

A focus on *doing* results in diminishing (killing) our *being*. Baptist author and church consultant Robert Dale said, "Our congregations can do so many good activities for God and his creatures that we lose the sense of being God's creatures and co-workers. Doing without being is deadening."

When I am "over-doing it" (which is easy for me to do) I am fractured, stressed, less productive and far from God. On the other hand, when I live out of who I am as a person and focus on *being,* I am centered, confident and energized. That kind of living results in the greatest *doing* (fruit) I can ever achieve.

Learn To Be

Shakespeare's Hamlet exclaimed, "To be, or not to be: that is the question." How do we grow in our *being*? How do we move from a *doing* focus to a *being* focus? If we are to grow in our *being*, we must start with the following.

Be God's Child. The Army's motto is, "Be all you can be." The way to *be all you can be* is found only in the Lord. In Ephesians the scriptures declare, *"It's in Christ that we find out who we are and what we are living for."* The place to begin *being* is by simply *being* God's child. Before we are a pastor, we are God's child. Before we are a husband and father, we are God's child. Our *being* (as a person and pastor) begins and ends in our relationship with Jesus. Relax and learn to be God's child. Let His grace engulf you. Let His power carry you. Focus on pleasing the Lord over others and you will experience peace in your *being*.

The world says we are what we produce. Our value is measured by our output. It is an assembly line mentality. How many parts can you slap on vehicles in a day? How many did you have in worship last Sunday? How many did you baptize last year? But the Lord says we have eternal value simply because we are His! The moment a baby is born mommy and daddy love that child completely. The baby hasn't done anything. The baby hasn't produced anything (other than tears, poop and spit up). Yet, mommy and daddy love their baby with every part of their being. They place supreme value on *their* baby.

Sometimes we are so busy *doing* the work of a pastor; we forget to *be* God's child. Take some time and just *be* God's child. Reflect on what it means to belong to God.

Know Yourself. We must be relentless in understanding and knowing ourselves. Knowing who we are as a person is essential to becoming the best we can be. This involves understanding our family of origin and the forces that helped shape our early lives. It involves studying and understanding our feelings, our personality type, what wears us out and what gives us energy. It entails facing and coming to grips with our insecurities (we all have them), our fears and our neuroses (we all have these as well). To know ourselves is to know the spiritual gifts God has given us and how those gifts should be applied. It involves being tested and knowing that we can survive and thrive when the going gets tough. Plato said, "The unexamined life is not worth living."

My wife, Robbi, is a strong extrovert and loves being around people. She gets her energy from being with people. I am slightly toward the introverted side. I love people, but if I am constantly around people, I get "peopled out." I need to go off by myself and read or do something private to re-energize. When we were first married this difference created tension in our relationship. I would come home from church after being around people all day and need some personal time. If I went off to another room to read or relax by myself for a little while, Robbi thought I was mad at her. As we studied personality types and understood our differences, this behavior and the tension it created in our marriage made sense. Now, it is not unusual for Robbi to see that I am stressed or worn out and say, "Mike, go to your room!"

Knowing yourself involves a humility that prays, "God, if I am going to be the best me that I can be, I must let You do Your complete work in every area of my life. I know this will not be easy. Your will be done."

Be Patient. It takes a lifetime for the Lord to shape us into the person He wants us to be. We are impatient. Always in a rush to get things done. Often we don't think about what we're *doing* or the value of what we are *doing*. We just *do* it. Since culture is focused on *doing*, we measure our lives by how much stuff we do. In *Experiencing God,* Henry Blackaby points out that we often hear the phrase, "Don't just stand there—do something." As he challenges us to experience God, Blackaby admonishes us to, "Don't just do something—stand there." The Heavenly Father took thirty years to shape the Son before He was ready for public ministry. Moses thought God had forgotten him. He spent forty years tending his father-in-law's flocks on the back side of the desert. God was shaping Moses into the person and leader Moses needed to be so he would be ready for the big job God had planned for him. From Paul's conversion on the road to Damascus, until he was ready to be the "apostle to the gentiles" took many years. God needed time to shape Paul into *someone*, before he was ready to do *something*.

I have a pastor friend in another part of the state who recently went through a tough experience. It was an experience most pastors encounter sometime in their ministry. My friend has been at his current church for many years. Recently, he felt an increasing interest to move to another church. He was courted by a church that appeared to be a perfect match for him. After being one of the finalists for this church, the chairman of the pastor search committee called to tell him they were no longer considering him. My friend called me to share his frustration and disappointment. Toward the end of our conversation he said, "Through this experience, the Lord is teaching me that it isn't nearly as important *where* I minister as *how* I minister."

I've noticed the Lord is calling fewer and fewer young men into the pastorate these days. Most of those entering the pastorate are older with several years of life and ministry experience. God is first shaping young ministers to *be* who he wants them to *be* before he sets them *doing* what he's called them to *do*.

Be Yourself. In the movie *Forrest Gump* Jenny asks, "Forrest, what you gonna be when you grow up?" With a confused look on his face, Forrest answers, "Can't I be me?" As a boy, I wanted to be like my Dad. And so I walked like my Dad, talked like my Dad, stood like my Dad and I even tried to shoot a basketball like my Dad even though I'm right handed and Dad is left handed. That kind of behavior is all right for a boy. But as I became a man, I needed to stand on my own two feet and be my own person. Pastors are notorious for imitating other pastors. For some reason (maybe because of our insecurities), we feel the need to preach like some preacher we have seen or comb our hair like some famous pastor or even dress like a pastor we admire. One thing I love to do at Baptist conventions is discover the trendy sport coat for pastors that year. Is it lime green, burgundy, tweed with patches on the sleeves or something different? Whatever it is you can be sure that a significant number of pastors have gotten the word and made sure they bought one before the convention. When Billy Graham preached his first Crusade in Dallas, Texas lots of Southwestern Seminary students went to hear him. In those days Billy preached from a big bright red Bible. They say that after the Graham Crusade, you couldn't find a red Bible in Ft. Worth. Southwestern students had bought them out.

Hosea's Experience

Hosea Bilyeu (Ridgecrest) tells a story about the time the Lord reminded him to be himself. Ridgecrest was growing significantly and Hosea was re-thinking his identity as a pastor.

> I thought "big church" pastors acted like "big church" pastors, without knowing what that meant and without feeling any different in my heart. Some things I was reading and hearing seemed to suggest that Senior Pastors should dress in certain ways and spend time with certain people, and I was at least wondering if I needed to be different.

During this period of struggle, Scotty Killingsworth (Evergreen), who was then pastor at Halltown, invited Hosea to come and preach a revival. A lady in Scotty's church knew Hosea from when he was a boy. Her family owned land next to the Bilyeu family property along Bull Creek. One night during the revival this lady gave Hosea a rock from Bull Creek.

I think she really thought it was a good luck piece. She told me she loved me and wanted me to have it. I took the rock and slipped it in my pocket. God used the rock to remind me of who I was (and am): a Bull Creek Country Boy! I left it in my pocket for months, and I still have the rock. I am proud of my hillbilly heritage, and am thankful for God's reminder.

Abraham Lincoln once stated, "I don't know who my grandfather was; I'm much more concerned to know what his grandson will be." Our most important job is to *be* who God created, saved, gifted and called us to *be*. I am to *be* the best me that I can *be*. You are to *be* the best you that you can *be*.

Caught More Than Taught

We can learn a lot about *being* by reading, studying and attending training conferences that emphasize a *being* focus in life. The best way to learn how to *be* is by observing others who live a *being* focus and live who they are. Look around for models and mentors who will not only tell you how to *be* but will show you the thrill of living out of your *being*.

I was blessed to grow up with parents who know how to *be* and who live a *being* focus. Mom is loving, gentle and very generous. Throughout her life, she has given herself to the care and nurture of others. Because of her gifts and her immense capacity to love, she kept foster kids, foreign exchange students, single women and many others in the home. She especially felt a call to help hurting or abused women. After a long teaching career, she taught GED classes for several years. Through her teaching, she met and helped numerous women finish their GED and get established in a job. She has been directly involved in helping women get their college degrees and go into the teaching profession. At seventy-nine years of age, Mom still tutors children, keeps children after school, manages the Salvation Army food pantry in her town, counsels women in need and helps in a nursing home ministry with Dad.

Dad is a thinker and learner. He loves to analyze things. He is a good chess player, reads biographies, theology and the New Testament in Greek. He is focused and loyal. At eighty years of age, he still helps his grandkids financially with their college and graduate degree expenses. Following many years as a pastor, teacher and high school principal, he served for several years on the local school board. He started a ministry in the county jail in Vinita, Oklahoma. Every Sunday afternoon he goes to the jail, leads services and counsels the men who seek him out. Regardless of the weather, nearly every day Dad takes his bird dog for a two mile walk in the neighborhood.

As I began to wrestle with the tension between a *doing* focus and a *being* focus in my life, I realized my parents were perfect models. Observe the people in your life. Learn from those who know how to *be*.

Hobbits

In the introduction to J.R.R. Tolkien's *The Hobbit* there is a revealing description of Hobbits. It says, "Hobbits are little people …they love peace and quiet and good tilled earth…they are nimble but don't like to hurry…they like to laugh and eat (six meals a day)…they like parties and they like to give and receive presents." I think Hobbits got it. They understood that to focus on *being* is the higher road in life. To live out of your *being* is to live a full and joyful life. The Hobbits were the lowly and forgotten people of Middle-Earth. They were small and weak and referred to as Halflings. However, the Hobbits were chosen as the ones to do the supreme job. Frodo and his friends were the ones who had the character and discipline to carry the ring to its necessary destination and in so doing they saved their people and Middle-Earth.

Leo Tolstoy said, "If you want to be happy, be."

The Key Is To Be

The key is to *be*. As we grow to *be* who God made us to *be*, we will achieve the divine purposes for which God gave us life. It's true that, "The wealthy man is the man who *is* much, not the man who *has* much."

If you take away anything from this chapter, remember this truth: *People, circumstances and your own limitations may keep you from **doing** something you want to do, but no one or nothing can keep you from **being** who God wants you to be.*

Chapter Two

YOUR CHURCH'S TOP PRIORITY

What is your church's number one priority? Is it your location and buildings? Vibrant worship? A powerful evangelism program? Perhaps it is a dynamic children's, youth or senior adult ministry. Better yet, maybe it is your preaching ministry. What is it?

I suggest your church's top priority is something entirely different. It is something that, if neglected, will have devastating consequences for your church. On the other hand, if this priority is given appropriate energy and attention, it will result in unimaginable blessings for your church and eternal benefits for God's Kingdom.

I believe your church's top priority is *your* (pastor's) personal walk with the Lord. As pastor, your relationship with Jesus is more vital to your church's health and ministry than anything else. It is more important than any program the church offers. More important than the resources (money, facilities, etc.) your church has. More important than the quality of your lay leadership. More important than your church's location. More important than anything! If you have a strong and growing relationship with the Lord, your church has its best chance to hear from God, place its priorities in order and truly be on mission for God. If you don't have a healthy and dynamic walk with God, then your church has little chance for effective advancement.

I heard of a successful pastor who was about to retire. A friend asked him to share his retirement plans. The old pastor said, "The first thing I'm going to do after I retire is get my life right with God." Many people would gasp in horror that a pastor would say such a thing. Pastors understand.

Advocate for Self

A pastor's work actually hinders a pastor from developing and maintaining a close relationship with the Lord. When you add up the preaching, teaching, visiting, administrating, care-giving, leading, relating, problem solving, writing, planning, wedding, funeraling (that's not a word), etc. a pastor does, there is no time left for a dynamic relationship with God.

On top of all the legitimate responsibilities, are all the unrealistic and unbiblical expectations church members pile on a pastor. It's enough to make a guy want to retire if for no other reason than to work on his relationship with the Lord.

Few pastors have anyone in their church who is an advocate for them to have the time, freedom and resources necessary to seriously work on their relationship with the Lord. *Pastors must advocate for themselves.* We must stand up for ourselves (and our churches) by insisting that we have what we need to build the relationship with the Lord that is required for our personal spiritual growth and the church's good. When I took that responsibility to heart and began carving out time for myself to be with God, it revolutionized my ministry and my church. Also, when I advocated for myself, support followed.

On one occasion, I planned a three day personal retreat away from the church. It was to be a time of spiritual renewal and planning. Before I left, I told several church leaders what I was doing. They were excited and promised to pray for me. One said, "There is one thing that I especially want you to do on this retreat. Get plenty of rest." With a lump in my throat, I promised I would.

Jesus Is Our Model

The Lord Jesus is our model. Several times in the Gospel of Mark we see where Jesus was under severe pressure and yet He carved out time to be alone with the Father.

One time people were bringing the sick and demon-possessed to Jesus and we read, *"The whole town gathered at the door."* Have you ever felt the whole town was gathered at your door? What did you do? Did you try to make sure everyone's needs were met? Did you try to make sure everyone left in good spirits so no one would criticize you? Did you try to help everyone so everybody would like you? If that's the case, you are probably barely surviving in your church. If that is how you operate, the leadership and ministry you give your church are far from your best. One of my spiritual heroes, Major Ian Thomas wrote, "There are a thousand needs, but you are not committed to these. You are committed to Christ, and it is His business to commit you where He wants you."

The scripture goes on to say the morning after Jesus healed the sick and demon-possessed He, *"Got up, left the house and went off to a solitary place, where he prayed."* Why did Jesus leave the house? Why didn't He stay there to pray? Jesus knew that in a brief time the *"whole town"* would gather at the door again. The only way He was going to get quality time with the Father was to get away. He took matters into His own hands. He advocated for Himself. He went away to a place where He could have some peace and quiet and spend time with His Father.

On another occasion, Jesus had just finished feeding the five thousand. People were coming from everywhere to hear Him and get a taste of what He and the disciples were dishing out. Jesus was on a roll. He was the most popular show in town. With the right public relations firm promoting Him, there was no telling how far He could go. But wait, Jesus had other plans. At the peak of His popularity Mark records, *"Immediately Jesus made his disciples get into the boat and go on ahead of him to Bethsaida, while he dismissed the crowd. After leaving them, he went up on a mountainside to pray."*

Jesus realized even success can distract us from our most important task. If we aren't careful, we will bask in our success and neglect needed time with the Father. There are times when we must do like Jesus and *"dismiss the crowd"* and tell those closest to us to *"go on ahead"* so we can have time and space to meet with God.

Most Important

Pastor, *you* are the *most important **human resource*** God gives your church. That means other than the *Scriptures* and the *Holy Spirit* you are the most important resource God gives your church. Think about that. Let it soak in. Again, *you*, as pastor of your church, are the *most important **human resource*** God gives your church. Your church may have a prime piece of real estate and beautiful facilities. You are more important. Your church may have a dynamic worship ministry. You are more important. Your church may have an outstanding evangelism program. You are more important. Your church may have excellent children's, youth and senior adult ministries. You are more important. You are unique. You have been gifted, called and strategically placed in your church for God's divine and eternal purposes. No other person on earth can do what you have been assigned to do. You are *essential* to the health and success of your church. It is imperative that you stay close to the One who led you to pastor your church. *Nothing* is more important to your church than *your* relationship with the Lord.

Deep Roots

Here's the problem. To spend time nurturing and growing your relationship with the Lord takes time. You have to take your hand off the plow of *doing* ministry if you are going to spend time *being* God's child and building your relationship with Him. As a pastor, you sometimes need to neglect the good of *doing* ministry so you can experience the best and *be* with God.

However, as a pastor, you long to see fruit in your ministry. You live and breathe to see people come to Christ, families healed, Christians thrive, hurting people find help and the Kingdom grow. Your experience has taught you that fruit comes from plowing and sowing and watering and weeding and harvesting. Doesn't it?

I was once deep in the Ozark woods spending time with the Lord. I noticed a towering oak tree and began admiring its massive trunk and long limbs. It dominated that part of the woods. I wondered how many droughts, storms and floods it survived. As I was looking up at the oak tree, I asked myself, "How does a tree grow that big and strong as well as bear that much fruit." There was evidence of its fruitfulness throughout the woods where I saw an abundance of other oak trees as well as acorns all over the ground. As soon as I asked the question, I knew the answer—*deep roots.* Only with *deep roots* does an oak tree have the foundation to grow big and bear fruit, much less withstand the wind, cold, storms and other forces that come against it.

Pastor, how is the root system in your life? Do you have roots that go deep in the Lord? Roots that tap into the living water of God's freshness, joy and purpose? Roots that wrap around the Rock of Ages, securing you to the stability and power of God? If not, you will be susceptible to every wind of difficulty that blows against you. Your life (and church) will bear little lasting fruit for God and His Kingdom.

As an old man, the great Methodist missionary E. Stanley Jones had a stroke that left him weak and almost speechless. While in that condition, Jones declared, "I need no outer props to hold up my faith for my faith holds me…Fortunately, with me, surrender to Jesus was the primary thing, and when the outer strands were cut by this stroke, my faith didn't shake." E. Stanley Jones had deep roots in the Lord. He was an oak tree for God.

Jesus said, *"Remain in me, and I will remain in you. No branch can bear fruit by itself; it must remain in the vine. Neither can you bear fruit unless you remain in me."*

Do you want joy in your life and fruit in your ministry? Do you want victory over temptation, strength to face and overcome trials, wisdom to make good ministry decisions and confidence to carry out those decisions? Then you must develop a deep root system that goes way down into the heart and soul of God.

Developing that type of root system is not easy. It takes work, determination, long-term commitment and sacrifice. It is a great temptation to put our roots into the Lord to a certain level and then stop and simply live and serve at that depth. I'm afraid that is what the majority of pastors do. As a result, our ministries are stale and shallow.

Fruit that Lasts

The story is told that one evening the great nineteenth century evangelist D. L. Moody was walking down a street in Chicago. He was approached by a drunk who asked him for money. As the drunk got close to Moody, he exclaimed, "I know you, I'm one of your converts." Moody retorted, "You must be one of mine, because you surely aren't the Lord's." As a pastor, you have experienced that kind of disappointment. We all have. We have produced fruit that was the result of our own hard work and then seen that fruit disappear in a flash revealing our wasted efforts.

How do we develop deep roots that bear lasting fruit? How do we grow a thriving relationship with the Lord that results in a strong and vibrant church? The scriptures teach that the development of a deep walk with God is a life-long endeavor.

Let me begin the following thoughts with a confession. My walk with God is up and down. It has never been a steady move upward (or forward). I've experienced many starts and stops, dry spells, growing times, plateaus and times in the wilderness. At this point in my life, my walk with God is strong and growing. But I know for a fact it won't always remain that way. That is the reality of being a sinful human in an imperfect world.

Responsibility

My relationship with the Lord is my responsibility. No one else can do this for me. No one else can say "no" to the myriad responsibilities that press against me so I can be with the Lord. No one else can discipline themselves to get up early or turn off the television or put down the newspaper or turn off the computer and go to a quiet place to spend intimate time with the Lord. Paul said, *"Work out your salvation with fear and trembling."* We are responsible for our own personal closeness (or distance) to God. It doesn't matter how many sermons we have to prepare or visits we have to make or meetings we have to attend or funerals we must perform. We are responsible. We can't blame a weak relationship with God on our church, family, denomination or anyone else. It is our fault. Once that is settled, we can get about the business of doing something about it.

Building Blocks

There are many building blocks to constructing a strong walk with God. These include prayer, the Bible, worship, meditation, fellowship with believers, accountability to others and service. It all begins with a love for God. In response to the Pharisee's question regarding the greatest commandment Jesus said, *"Love the Lord your God with all your heart and with all your soul and with all your mind. This is the first and greatest commandment."* Without love, our relationship with the Lord isn't going anywhere. It doesn't matter how much time we spend with Him or what we do. Everything must be undergirded with a deep and humble love. This means our motivation for building a relationship with God is not so we can get something from Him (selfish) or bear fruit (manipulation), but that we might know Him and live in light of His grace and will.

I was a freshman in high school when I met a university student who helped me in my walk with God. He had a contagious relationship with the Lord and it spilled over on me. Through our conversations, he told me he had a special time of meeting with God that he called his "quiet time." I think it was the first time I ever heard that phrase. It made sense. The idea stuck. Some years later I followed his counsel and began having a regular time of prayer, Bible reading and fellowship with the Lord. Since then, I've been faithful to a special time with the Lord. That time is essential to my growth and walk with Christ. Do I ever miss a day? Sure I do. I'm more concerned that my walk with God is sincere and real than I am about conforming to a daily ritual.

Intimate relationships take privacy and time. There are no short-cuts here. Imagine trying to understand your wife's deepest needs and talking with her about important things while others are standing at your shoulder clamoring for your attention. Imagine trying to talk with your wife about future family plans and dreams while the room is filled with other people. Imagine trying to have a romantic rendezvous with your sweetheart while others are nearby! Well, you get the picture. If you want to be close to someone, you must have time alone.

Pathways

In Gary Thomas' book, *Sacred Pathways,* he discusses the various ways people connect with God. Some enjoy nature, others prefer in-depth Bible study and still others are inspired by music. We need to know ourselves and discover the pathways that are natural and helpful avenues for us to connect with God.

Let me share a few of the pathways that are most helpful to me. If I neglect these, my walk with God suffers.

A Place. I need a special place where I can get alone with God. An old chair that sits in the corner of a guest bedroom in our home is that place for me. I keep my Bible, journal, books, prayer list, hymn book and other stuff on the floor beside the chair. If I'm not careful, it gets cluttered and Robbi lets me know about it. That place is sacred to me.

Prayer. As I sit in (or sometimes kneel beside) that chair, I open myself to the Lord and pray. I have a prayer list, but oftentimes I just pray what is on my heart and mind. I also listen. I believe prayer is primarily a frame of mind and an open heart. Once we are in the right spirit, we connect and converse with God. Prayer lists are beneficial, but we need to be careful that our goal is not just to recite a list, but to connect with the Father. There is one list I pray through nearly every Sunday morning. That is the list of pastors and churches in the Association.

Bible. The Bible is God's holy, inspired Word. As we read and study the Bible, God reveals Himself and His will to us. Throughout the years, I've read through the Bible many times in several different translations. At present, I am going through the scriptures and making my own annotated Bible. I summarize the text by writing in the margins of my Bible. Spending significant time in scripture is necessary for building a strong relationship with God.

Journaling. I started journaling thirty years ago. About twenty years ago I began journaling consistently. Journaling helps me record thoughts, struggles, fears, thanks, prayers, family experiences, failures, successes, progress and lessons God is teaching me. It helps to write it down. I love to go back and read answers to prayer. It's encouraging when I read and re-read how the Lord brought me through tough times. I believe the scriptures are God's journals He shares with us. In Exodus we read, *"Moses then wrote down everything the Lord had said."* We take pictures to record vacations and family reunions and we keep cards and letters that have special meaning. If God journals (Bible), it only makes sense that part of my spiritual growth would involve journaling.

Singing. Singing to the Lord helps me feel God's grace and pleasure. I like to use the Baptist Hymnal. I just flip through the pages until I find a hymn that seems right and then I sing it to the Lord. When I lift my feeble voice to God my heart soars with joy and thanksgiving. My voice isn't anything like the voices of some of the pastors in our Association. But, when I'm alone with God and I raise my voice in praise, God hears and I sense His presence, experience His blessing and feel His pleasure.

Nature. I love the Ozarks and I love being out in nature. I have a little hobby that I started not long after Robbi and I moved to Springfield. I visit the beautiful springs we have in Southwest

Missouri and take pictures of them. I have put together a couple of scrapbooks with pictures of springs along with clippings of the springs I've accumulated from magazines and newspapers. Have you ever been to Alley Spring in Shannon County and watched the water bubble up in the turquoise pool and then rush down to the Jacks Fork? What about Hodson Mill Spring in Ozark County? It is one of the most exquisite spots in the state (or nation). The water comes rushing out of the mill into a pond where it then spills over a waterfall and flows into Bryant Creek. Or, have you been to Greer Springs in Oregon County? This is my favorite. The spring gushes out of a cave and then roars down the valley connecting with the Eleven Point River. When I'm in nature I sense the majesty and power of God.

Solitude. Gary Thomas observed that, "Cultivating the quiet is a painful experience when we are addicted to noise, excitement, and occupation." Years ago I discovered that I must get away for significant time alone with the Lord. This discipline helps me draw closer to the Lord more than anything else I do. I love my work. However, I feel stress deeply. Over time, stress sticks to me like lint on a pair of wool slacks. It's like I walk around collecting more and more lint (stress) until it weighs me down and I can't move. The only way for me to truly unwind and clean off the stress is to get away. Assumption Abbey near Ava has become my solitude refuge. Whether I stay in my room praying and reading, walk in the woods or sit in a prayer service and listen to the monks chant the Psalms, I feel a closeness to the Lord I rarely feel at other times.

Fasting. Fasting is a way for me to focus and hear from God. I don't fast often. But, I will fast if there is a major decision I need to make. Fasting helps me get things in proper perspective, humble myself before the Lord, acknowledge His Lordship and listen. On several occasions the Lord has led me to make critical decisions that were revealed during a fast. Several years ago, I conducted a week-long fast where all I took in was water or juice. During that fast, I felt the leading of the Lord to invite Samuel González to join our Associational staff. God has honored and blessed that decision in ways only He knows. Samuel is a great blessing to our Association and our churches.

These are some of the pathways that benefit me in my walk with God. What feeds your soul? What pathways draw you close to the Lord? Know yourself and develop habits that help you build a dynamic walk with God.

Your Church Depends On It

The pressures and pace of the pastorate make it difficult for pastors to build and maintain an intimate walk with God. Pastor, *you* are the *most important **human resource*** God gives your church. The health and vitality of your church depends on the strength of your walk with God. Let nothing or no one keep you from the Lord. Your church and His Kingdom depend on it!

Chapter Three

CHERISH YOUR FAMILY

When my daughter Heidi was eight years old she wrote me a special note. It was written on pink Hello Kitty stationery and placed in a pink Hello Kitty envelope. For years, I kept the note on the dashboard of my car to remind me of what is important in life. Heidi wrote this note at a particularly stressful period in my church. A period when I neglected my children while thinking I was being a faithful pastor. In Heidi's eight year old printing she wrote this to me, *"Dear Dad, I love you so much, but you need to talk more to us. Love, Heidi."*

One time I was reflecting on how to balance a successful busy pastorate with the needs of young children. How could I spend the time and energy necessary to grow my church and at the same time spend a healthy amount of time with my kids? I remember thinking that every parent can't spend a fair amount of time with their kids. Some parents have such critical work (calling) that they may need to neglect their kids for a greater good. If their kids turned out badly, then that is tough. That may be the sacrifice necessary for their work (calling) to be done with excellence. I suddenly jerked myself together and thought, "Mike, that is the most ridiculous thought you ever had. That's stupid!"

Pastor, your wife and kids are God's precious gift to you. Do not let anything (anything!) stand between you and a wonderful relationship with your family. You must cherish your family. If your relationship with your wife and kids is not vibrant, your walk with God will be weak. If your relationship with your wife and kids is not growing, your ministry will suffer.

Inter-Connected Whole

Life is an interdependent, inter-connected whole. We like to think we can divide life into different categories or sub-groups and deal with them separately. We want to believe we have our ministry or church work in a certain place. In another place we have sports and hobbies. Still in another place we have our family. And maybe in another place we have our denominational work or school. We try to isolate and deal with issues and problems in one area of life and not let it affect the others. We can't. Whatever affects one part influences the whole. Whatever hurts the toenail on your little toe or the muscles in your lower back has immediate and serious effect on your entire body. Those hurts affect what you think, how you feel, what you say (or yell) and literally everything related to your self.

Prior to a recent mission trip to India, I hurt the muscles in my lower back. I did it while over-doing my exercise routine. I went to the doctor and got pain medicine and muscle relaxants. The medicines didn't help much. I tried to isolate the pain and go on as if it didn't exist. I did everything I could to ignore it. I tried to tough it out. I even told myself it wouldn't affect the trip. I was fooling myself. The sixteen hour plane trip from Chicago to New Delhi was the most miserable sixteen hours I ever spent. Whatever I did to try to compartmentalize my pain only served to remind me that my body is an inter-connected whole and what hurts or affects one part has immediate and profound effect on all parts. Fortunately, with Robbi by my side and great leadership on the trip, we had a wonderful and fruitful time.

Give Your Best

Our relationship with and care of our family has profound impact on every part of our lives. It is imperative we give our family our best. Paul wrote these words to Pastor Timothy, *"Here is a trustworthy saying: If anyone sets his heart on being an overseer*

...He must manage his own family well and see that his children obey him with proper respect. If anyone does not know how to manage his own family, how can he take care of God's church?" How does a pastor do that? How does a pastor care for his church and do everything a local pastor has to do while effectively caring for his family?

As a husband and father (and especially as a pastor), you must serve your wife and children and give them your best. Don't give them your leftovers. Don't toss them your crumbs after you used yourself up at church. Don't come home with zero energy for your family because you used it all up on church members. Talk to your wife. Listen to your children. Make exciting plans together. Pray with them. Spend lots of time with them. Study and know your wife. Understand your kids. Learn their personality types, their likes and dislikes, what they love to do and what they want to do with you. Many pastors know more about the Gospel of John, the life of Martin Luther or the latest Baptist political maneuverings than they do about their wife and kids. What does your wife enjoy? When your kids are alone, what do they think about? What makes your wife laugh? What are your children's deepest longings?

Love Her

Paul admonishes husbands to, *"Love your wives, just as Christ loves the church...he who loves his wife loves himself."* Paul concludes these thoughts by saying that when a husband and wife come together they are *"one flesh."* In another place, Paul teaches that the bodies of husbands and wives literally belong to the spouse. Our lives are linked, joined and even fused to others far beyond our awareness. Again, whatever happens to one part of our lives affects the whole. If we neglect or mistreat our family, it will have devastating consequences on our walk with God and ministry.

I had a good friend in seminary whose wife took their kids and left him. My friend was distraught. His wife told him that she loved him, but she didn't want to be married to a pastor. He agonized over what he should do. He felt a clear call to ministry, but he also knew the scriptural mandates to love and support his family. He decided he had to do everything possible to salvage his marriage and regain his family. He quit seminary, gave away his library (some to me) and moved to live near his family. Over time, he and his wife were reconciled and his family restored. The last thing I heard was that he was an administrator in a Christian school and his family was doing well.

I believe my friend did the right thing. First, the Lord calls us to *be somebody* ahead of *doing some things*. In other words, we are called to cherish our family above our call to pastor a local church. Is this a conflict? I don't think so. My friend didn't give up his call to ministry. He continued to serve the Lord faithfully and was able to use his gifts to bless others and build the Kingdom. He simply did it in a different venue. He served in a Christian school rather than as a pastor.

Pastor, how do you need to demonstrate your love for your wife beyond what you are already doing? Does she know how precious she is to you? Your wife needs to see your love. She sees you love others in the church by your acts of ministry. How has she seen your love for her lately?

Know Her

I was attracted to Robbi for obvious reasons. She is beautiful, loves life, wants her life to be used by God to bless others and has an infectious laugh. As I got to know her, I wanted to know more about her. I was not satisfied to simply know her at the level of my initial attraction. That longing to know her better and to understand her more fully has not diminished. In fact, it grows as we grow in our love.

Many years ago I wrote the following in my journal: "Robbi is the perfect wife for me. She is exciting and expressive which balances my mild-mannered blahness. Ha! She is her own woman with strong opinions. She loves the Lord but won't be placed in a box through her service or church involvement. She is a great encourager—which I need. She gives my life a flair no other woman could give it. She is a great mother and challenges me to be the best Dad I can be. She's stimulating to me intellectually. She believes in me. She's a wonderful lover! I'm so fortunate to have her, Lord. Thank you—praise your name! May our next years be even better."

Empower Her

If a husband truly loves his wife, he will help her be herself. This is a challenge for pastors' wives. Many church members have ridiculous expectations of their pastor's wife. They have a picture of the perfect pastor's wife in their minds; an image with expectations no person can fulfill. Pastors need to protect their wives from these intrusive expectations. They must help their wives be themselves while helping church members accept an appropriate role for their wife.

A pastor in our Association recently told me the following experience. During the Christmas season, he attended a Sunday School party at the home of a church member. A little old lady approached him during the party and demanded, "Where's your wife?" He explained that she was away taking care of her aging parents. The lady responded with, "Well, she should be here with you." The pastor told me he didn't argue with the lady, but clearly let her know that his wife was doing exactly what she was supposed to do and was where she was supposed to be.

Robbi doesn't play the piano. On more than one occasion, the first question she was asked by a pastor search committee was, "Do you play the piano?" It made her feel like a failure as a pastor's wife. Robbi has wonderful gifts and abilities in administration, leadership, relationship building, teaching and serving. In each church where I served as pastor the Lord used her gifts in ways that made a great impact for the Kingdom. God used her to start Sunday School departments and classes, create outreach ministries, grow young adults in faith and service and do a myriad of other vital things. These were the results of using her own particular gifts in exactly the way God intended. Not according to the desires (or complaints) of church members.

Mature church members understand the pastor's wife is neither an extension of her husband nor is she there to fill the narrow expectations of some people in the church. They realize the pastor's wife is her own person with her own interests and gifts and is free to find her own place of service in the church.

Protect Her

The most important role of the pastor's wife is simply to be the pastor's wife. If she does nothing more for the church than love and support her husband, she will be successful as a pastor's wife. Pastors must be certain they give their wives the freedom and blessing to do that. Pastors themselves often place unhealthy and inappropriate expectations on their wives. If the church needs another children's worker, nursery volunteer, or youth event sponsor the pastor looks to his wife to fill the gap. Then he complains she doesn't have energy or enthusiasm for the home, kids or him.

Pastor, let your wife be herself. Encourage her to serve where she is gifted and feels called. Or, not serve actively in any formal position, but focus on encouraging and supporting you. Protect her from the inappropriate expectations of church members. You will be blessed by the joy she will give the family and the energy she gives you for ministry. The one car bumper sticker that is absolutely true is, "If Momma Ain't Happy, Ain't Nobody Happy!"

Sabbath

Pastor, give your wife a Sabbath. The fourth commandment is the one pastors and their wives break consistently. It is the one that says, *"Remember the Sabbath day by keeping it holy. Six days you shall labor and do all your work, but the seventh day is a Sabbath to the Lord your God. On it you shall not do any work..."* We have made the Sabbath commandment about worship and going to church. I don't deny that is a part of it. But what is the primary purpose of the Sabbath? What is the principle that underlies the commandment? It is not church attendance. It is rest. Jesus said, *"The Sabbath was made for man, not man for the Sabbath."* God made us to need rest. The Sabbath commandment is a key provision to make sure we get it. If we neglect our rest, we are weakened. As a result, we will fall short of *being* and *doing* our best for God.

Pastor, when does your wife get a Sabbath? If she works outside the home or has other weekday responsibilities (such as home-schooling children), she doesn't get a Sabbath during the week. Saturdays are typically wild and crazy with family, community and church responsibilities. And Sunday? Forget it! So, pastor, when does your wife get a Sabbath? Is there anything you can do to insure she does?

You can do many things to help your wife in this area. You can assist around the house, take the kids out on Saturday so she has some time alone at home or encourage her to go out with friends. Make sure the two of you spend special time together doing things she enjoys whether that is a quiet evening at home, going out to dinner and a movie, going on a walk or working on some family or home project.

What if, on occasion, you gave your wife Wednesday night, Sunday night or (heaven forbid!) Sunday morning off? That's right, what if you sometimes said, "Honey, this has been an extremely busy time and I know you are under a lot of stress. I'm going to take the kids to church and I want you to stay home and do whatever you want." How would your wife react? How would that impact her relationship with you? Would that let her know that she is more important to you than the church? I remember one time I did this for Robbi (I've done this several times for her). When I got back from church she told me she enjoyed the best personal time with the Lord she remembered having in a long time. That is Sabbath.

Don't Exasperate Children

After Paul tells husbands to love their wives he says, *"Fathers, do not exasperate your children; instead, bring them up in the training and instruction of the Lord."* I like how it reads in The Message, *"Fathers, don't exasperate your children by coming down hard on them. Take them by the hand and lead them in the way of the Master."* This haunts me. I exasperated my children. Especially my eldest child Josh. When he was a teenager I was tough on him. At times, I took the stress I was experiencing at church out on him. I allowed my inner struggles to come out in anger toward him. I especially fussed at him about his school work and grades. Thankfully, I repented, he forgave me and we have a wonderful relationship today. But I know what it is to behave in a manner that exasperates your children. I'm concerned this type of behavior is common for pastors.

Pressure

First, we have the "call" of God on our lives. This creates high expectations and causes us to take ourselves way too seriously. Second, we want our family to model perfect Christian behavior. We want to get social and ministry mileage out of our kids' behavior. We think if our kids behave well, people will like us, trust us and follow our leadership. On the other hand, if our kids act badly, we will look bad and people won't trust us. Third, church members have unrealistic expectations of us and our family. Fourth, we live in a culture that increasingly looks at the church and pastors with suspicion or even disdain. All of this expectation and pressure puts the squeeze on us. This pressure must have an outlet. If we aren't aware of this and if we don't have positive ways to relieve the stress, it is likely to be directed at our families.

What's a pastor (and Father) to do? First and foremost, we must work on ourselves. This means focus on *being*. We must focus on *being* God's child and living in light of His grace. As we grow to be the man, husband and father God wants us to be, we give our families the best chance they have to *be* who God wants them to *be*. We must develop healthy outlets for the pressure that inevitably builds. This may be through exercise, a hobby, solitude or any number of ways. We must learn and grow through the pain and pressure of being a pastor.

God's Design

We need to enjoy our children and let them be who God designed them to be. This means we give them room to fail and grow. My son Josh loves sports. His life revolved around sports when he was in high school. Making good grades was on the low end of his priority list. He didn't fail. He just didn't perform up to his potential.

During his sophomore year, we began having serious father-son conflict. Much of the conflict revolved around his grades. I was constantly badgering him about his grades. I realized if I continued down that road it might severely damage our long-term relationship. I also realized my harping on him was more about my wanting him to do well so I could brag on him (social mileage) than it was about his learning and growing to be the best young man he could be.

After serious reflection, I decided I needed to change. I told Josh I would make a deal with him. I would back away and not gripe about his grades as long as he made at least "C's." In turn, if a grade dropped below a "C," he would seek my help and we would work to bring the grade up. We shook on it. That may have been the best parenting decision I made regarding Josh.

I kept my end of the bargain and so did he. I worked hard at not saying anything but positive comments about his grades. He came to me for help when he began having trouble in Algebra II. We worked together to make sure he got the grade up and both celebrated when he finished that semester with a "C." I'll never forget the morning I went to school with him to meet with his Algebra teacher. As we walked down the hall, I assumed he would be embarrassed to be seen with his Dad. But when his football and basketball buddies yelled down the hallway, "Josh, what's up?" He yelled back, "I'm having problems in Algebra and my Dad's helping me out. We're going to meet with my teacher." It was like he and I had this pact. I let him be his own young man, but when he needed help he would unashamedly ask for it.

The space I gave Josh to handle his own school work and make his own grades helped us have a much better relationship during his high school years. It also contributed to the great relationship we have today. Furthermore, the room I gave him helped him "own" his own school work which led to adequate grades in high school, good grades in college and excellent grades in graduate school.

Bless Your Kids

The greatest thing you can do for your kids is to bless them. Through your grace and blessing, you nurture them spiritually in better and deeper ways than any amount of family devotions could ever hope to achieve. The Message says, *"Fathers, don't exasperate your children by coming down hard on them. **Take them by the hand and lead them in the way of the Master.**"* Children long for the approval and blessing of their parents.

This was driven home to me when Josh and I were having our battles. One night I was griping about his school work and his failure to stay on top of his homework. He was testy and defensive. I yelled at him and told him there would be serious consequences if he didn't get his homework done right then. At that point, his eyes filled with tears and I thought, "There is something else going on here." I asked what was wrong and he shot back "nothing." I stormed out of the room and down the hall.

I was in another room working on a project and in a little while Josh came up behind me and started rubbing my shoulders. When I stood up and turned around I saw his eyes were full of tears. He told me that in biology class that day he worked especially hard on a project (dissecting a frog) and he just knew that he was going to get an excellent grade. He was proud of his work and was already looking forward to telling me about it and about the good grade he knew he would get. Well, when the teacher looked at his work he gave Josh a weak grade. He was disappointed in the grade and crushed that he couldn't give me a good report. When I realized how disappointed he was in letting me down I grabbed him, hugged him and we literally bawled in each others arms. I knew then that my attitude and behavior toward my son was wrong. More than anything else he wanted to please me. My demands for perfection were driving a wedge between us. Instead of Josh feeling grace and blessing from me, he felt disappointment, anger and failure.

I read recently that in work environments it takes three positive statements to offset one negative statement. In other words, negative statements are three times more powerful than positive statements. Why is the bad stuff easier to believe than the good stuff? Author Philip Yancey says we live in a culture of *ungrace.* We are constantly bombarded with messages of failure, disappointment and *ungrace.* I believe people (and especially children) are starving for grace. If our kids don't get grace and blessing from us, there will be a grace and blessing deficit in them for the rest of their lives.

In Yancey's book, *What's So Amazing About Grace,* he tells an Ernest Hemingway story about a Spanish father and his son Paco. The Father and Paco had a terrible falling out and Paco ran away to the great city of Madrid. The father was broken-hearted over the conflict and wanted to find his son and apologize. He didn't know how to get in touch with Paco so he took an ad out in the *El Liberal* newspaper. The ad said, "PACO, MEET ME AT HOTEL MONTANA NOON TUESDAY. ALL IS FORGIVEN. PAPA." Paco is a common name in Spain. Imagine Papa's amazement when he showed up at Hotel Montana and found eight hundred (800) Pacos waiting and hoping it was their Papa who was coming.

If you bless your children, they will bless you beyond your wildest dreams. I recently received a Hallmark Card from my daughter Heidi for my fifty-seventh birthday. The card says, "*Do you have any idea how many of my happiest memories involve you?*" Inside Heidi wrote, "*I love you Dad! I hope this is your best year yet. Love you. Heidi.*"

Example

More than anything else, our children want to be close to us. They long to be nurtured and taught by us. We have a spiritual responsibility and biblical mandate to "*Take them by the hand and lead them in the way of the Master.*" This doesn't mean we are to preach to them or cajole them to pray, read their Bible and so on. It begins by setting an example. It means *being* the person God made and gifted us to *be*. It means living life in God's grace and power.

I was a boy when I saw my Dad, early one morning, kneeling by his bed and praying. That scene of my Dad on his knees is vividly imprinted in my mind. Without question, that example has had a profound impact on my understanding of prayer, daily priorities and other vital aspects of life. We need to spend time reading the Bible and praying with our children, but more important than that our children need to see us doing those things on our own.

One way Robbi and I "*took our children by the hand*" was to regularly report answers to prayers during family devotions. When your children see their prayers answered, and see spiritual victories in the family, they want more.

The pastor's family has a unique opportunity. Through the church, you have the means to connect your children to spiritual giants. First, you do this by making sure your children are close to the spiritually mature people in the church. Second, you should take advantage of guest evangelists, Bible teachers and missionaries who come to your church by making sure your children get to know them and their life stories. Pastor, take your children by the hand and lead them in the way of the Master. Your church, your children and future generations will bless you for it.

Fun

You have heard the phrase, "The family that *prays* together stays together." Psychologists tell us, "The family that *plays* together stays together." One way to make sure you don't exasperate your children is to have fun with them. Healthy families have fun. When our kids were little Robbi and I decided we were going to be intentional about having fun. In fact, we said we wanted to have so much fun with our kids that even if they went wild and crazy when they left home, they would come back if for no other reason than for the fun. From our earliest years, we played table games, went to movies, went fishing, attended community and sports events, went on summer vacations, developed our own Christmas and birthday traditions and did a zillion other things. We created a monster! Now our kids, their spouses and our grandkids have so many fun things planned for the whole family that Robbi and I have to plan way ahead to squeeze in fun time for ourselves.

Isn't God good? The creation of the family was one of God's best ideas. Cherish your family.

Chapter Four

DON'T WASTE PAIN

How do you respond to adversity, problems and pain? This may be the most important question a Christian will face. Pastor, how do you respond to criticism? How do you handle church conflict? How do you react to physical adversity? How do you adjust to failure? What do you do with pain?

I'm talking about all types of pain: physical pain; emotional pain; and spiritual pain. Pain that is our fault, someone else's fault or no one's fault. Pain that God sends or simply permits.

James wrote, *"Consider it pure joy, my brothers, whenever you face trials of many kinds, because you know that the testing of your faith develops perseverance. Perseverance must finish its work so that you may be mature and complete, not lacking anything...Blessed is the man who perseveres under trial, because when he has stood the test, he will receive the crown of life that God has promised to those who love him."*

Pain is an opportunity. It is a word from God. Pain is a precious commodity that must not be wasted. We must take the pain that comes into our lives and squeeze every bit of good out of it we can. *Don't waste pain.*

Pain Is for Everyone

Notice James assumed everyone will face trials. *"My brothers"* refers to all those to whom the letter is written. Pain is for everyone. It is an equal opportunity offender. It is not prejudiced, selective or exclusive. Furthermore, pain is especially for the

Christian. Isn't that great to know! Paul declares, *"The Spirit himself testifies with our spirit that we are God's children. Now if we are children, then we are heirs—heirs of God and co-heirs with Christ, if indeed we share in his sufferings in order that we may also share in his glory."* If you are a child of God you will suffer. It is guaranteed. Pain is not an optional part of being a follower of Jesus. It comes with the territory.

During a television interview, I heard Roger Staubach, former quarterback for the Dallas Cowboys, asked how he continued playing professional football with all the injuries he suffered. Staubach said, "If you're not playing hurt, you're not playing football." The Bible says, if you're not living hurt, you're not living the Christian life.

My friend Morton Rose is an avid golfer. Morton believes every pastor should take up the game of golf if for no other reason than to learn to live with failure and pain.

Pain Happens

I was a twenty-one year old youth minister in Oklahoma when the Lord began to teach me about pain. I had faithfully served my church for eighteen months. It was the primary source of income for Robbi and me. We were four months away from graduating from college and I was fired.

Just like you, my life has been filled with both joy and pain. I've been married thirty-seven years. Robbi and I raised two children. I've pastored three churches; two of those churches were in transitional areas of downtown Kansas City, Missouri. I spent time in a hospital with a serious illness. I've had loved ones die. I've lived a full range of life which involves both joy and pain. Each one of you could give a similar story. Pain is for everyone.

Pastors and Pain

I love pastors. My calling is to bless, train and lead pastors. The pastor is the key to the success of his church. He is God's appointed spiritual leader of his congregation. If he is in tune with God and leading effectively, his church has an excellent chance to fulfill God's purposes. If he is *out of sync* with God or is leading poorly, his church has very little chance of success.

Pastors are in pain. The pain pastors experience today is the same pain prophets of old, the Apostles and even the Lord Jesus experienced. Pastor, you know you are hurting. See your pain in its larger context. Recognize you are not alone in your struggles.

In the second year of my third pastorate, things were not going well. Attendance was declining, we had no unified vision, church members openly questioned my leadership and the ministerial staff was angry with me. The staff decided we would have a Saturday morning retreat and talk things through. After the retreat, I recorded the following in my journal, "The four of us sat down to try to work through some of these differences…it became a "bash Mike" session. They feel my preaching stinks, I can't pastor and my administration style doesn't work."

It was about this time that I also recorded this statement in my journal. "There have been some times this past year when I felt as though no one was standing with me but the Lord. However, I discovered that if the only one I know (or feel) is supporting me is the Lord—that's enough!! I must never forget that!!"

Pastors under Attack

Pastors are under attack. There are several reasons for this. One is we live in a time when leaders are viewed with suspicion and skepticism. Another is that our culture is flowing away from the things of God and the church. There were periods in our nation's history when the flow of culture was toward the church. Not today.

We live in a quick-fix, blame-it-on-someone-else culture. When church attendance and offerings drop or there is tension in the church, people assume it is their pastor's fault.

Another reason pastors are under attack is the high level of anxiety in people's lives. This anxiety will find an outlet. People don't know how to appropriately deal with their anxiety. They are afraid to scream at their boss or pick a fight with a neighbor. So, they let their anger and frustrations out at the safest place possible—church. They beat up their pastor.

Of course, another reason pastors are under attack is the unbiblical and unrealistic expectations church members have of their pastor. It doesn't matter what a pastor does—somebody is going to be mad at him.

Finally (and underlying all the other reasons), the pastor is constantly on the front-lines of spiritual warfare. The enemy knows if the pastor is weakened or crippled, the church will fail.

The pastor is like a quarterback who is fighting to drive his team for a touchdown. The trouble is his offensive live is porous and he is always scrambling for his life. He doesn't have time to set his feet, much less get off a good pass.

As a pastor, you live with pain. It is imperative you understand pain and use it for your good and God's glory.

Face Pain

James says, *"Whenever you face trials."* That doesn't mean you go into each day looking for trouble. I read about a lady who got up one morning and put on a t-shirt with the words: "Be Nice To Me. I Had A Hard Day." Her young son read the t-shirt and asked, "Mommy, how can you tell this early in the morning?"

To *"face trials"* means we know they will come and when they do we look at them squarely. We see the pain. We acknowledge it. We feel it. Then we are able to address it and deal with it.

We live in a culture obsessed with getting rid of pain. If you can devise a pill or technique to alleviate a little pain you will get rich overnight. Our obsession with getting rid of pain limits our willingness to address pain and look at its deeper meaning. Is this pain a warning? Do I need to learn something from this pain? Where is God in this pain?

Our natural tendency is to escape. We take a pill or run away. If there are problems in the church, then church members move their membership to another church while the pastor updates his resume and sends it out to friends. I heard a pastor once say that if he could build the church of his dreams, he would build it with a trap door on the platform. At the conclusion of the Sunday morning worship service, he would look up and see who was coming toward him. If it was the little lady with her litany of physical ailments or the fellow with his list of complaints about the church, he could escape through the trap door.

From time to time, we all fantasize about escaping. I used to fantasize about being a toll booth operator on the Will Rogers Turnpike. Robbi and I are originally from Oklahoma and we still have lots of family in Oklahoma. While on vacation, we would invariably drive on the Will Rogers Turnpike. As I paid the toll booth operator, I would think, "Wow, what a job. The deepest relationship this operator has is to greet people or maybe give a warning about the road conditions and the most he/she has to think is how to make change for a dollar bill!" No offense to toll booth operators. We think all kinds of ridiculous stuff in our fantasies.

Sometimes it may be legitimate to escape. There may be occasions when you need to turn your back on pain and leave. Even Jesus said there are circumstances where you should, *"Shake the dust off your feet when you leave…"* I've known pastors in abusive church situations where it got so bad the best thing was for the pastor to take his family and leave. However, we must never do that until we face our pain and squeeze all the good out of it we can. Once we do that and have a release (or leading) from God, we can leave.

Jesus faced His pain squarely on the cross. No wavering or hesitancy. He dealt with it and worked through it. And we are forever grateful!

The Gift of Pain

Dr. Paul Brand was a marvelous Christian, world-renowned surgeon and leprosy specialist. He received the Surgeon General's Medallion for his work. Dr. Brand was the first one to attack the "bad flesh" belief about leprosy. This is the belief that the leprosy itself mysteriously causes the rotting or deterioration of the flesh that disfigures those with the disease of leprosy.

Dr. Brand theorized and proved that the bacilli virus, which causes leprosy, kills the nerve endings thus stopping pain. Without pain, those suffering with leprosy abuse their extremities. This leads to sores, infection and finally deterioration. In his book *The Gift of Pain,* Dr. Brand tells horrifying stories of how leprosy patients damage their bodies because they feel no pain. For example, they wear ill-fitting shoes that squeeze their toes and cut off blood circulation. When they cook meat over hot coals they use their hands to turn the meat instead of using tongs. They allow their bodies to get too cold and suffer frostbite.

Dr. Brand spent many years working in a leprosarium in Vellore, India. While working at the leprosarium, Dr. Brand spent a great deal of time and effort to discover the causes of the sores on his patients. Again, the conventional wisdom was they were caused by the disease itself. He tenaciously believed they were caused by abuses to the body that were the result of a lack of pain. Dr. Brand believed each of the sores and subsequent deterioration had simple explanations. He felt if they could watch the leprosy patients' normal daily routine, they would discover how they were abusing their bodies which led to the sores.

Several young leprosy patients assisted Dr. Brand in this research. They would follow other patients around making notes of their routines and attempting to discover how they were harming themselves. There was one particular type of injury it seemed they would never solve. Sometimes leprosy patients would awaken in the morning with open bloody wounds on the ends of their fingers. There seemed to be no explanation for these injuries. Finally, some of Dr. Brand's helpers stayed up all night to watch the patients and find out the cause of the injuries. To their horror, they discovered that during the night, rats would enter the bedrooms and chew on the ends of their fingers. Without pain, the patients slept soundly, not realizing what was happening. One young helper named Raman was distraught over this discovery. In tears he cried out, "Dr. Brand, how can I ever be free without pain?" Dr. Brand became a champion for pain. It was his mission to convince people that pain is a gift.

Pain *is* a gift. We don't want to hear that. We want to hear pain is evil, the enemy. James said, *"Consider it pure joy…whenever you face trials…"* Paul said, *"Rejoice in our sufferings…"* Peter said, *"Our trials will result in praise, glory and honor…"* Jesus said, *"Blessed are you when people insult you…rejoice and be glad…"*

What Is God Saying?

A friend was diagnosed with malignant cancer. He told me a persistent pain in his side led him to the doctor which led to the early diagnosis of his disease. He said, "I never thought of pain as my friend, but it was." The most precious and powerful saints I've known are those who responded to pain in humility. They grew through pain and because of pain.

Pain is God's primary tool to shape you to *be* the person He wants you to *be*. Do you realize God doesn't particularly care what you do? In the grand scheme of things *what you do* is not that important. However, God cares supremely about *who you are*. He will do whatever necessary, including allowing pain, to shape you into the person He wants you to *be*. As God makes you into whom He wants you to *be*, He will set you *doing* what He wants you to *do*.

Benjamin Franklin said, "The things which hurt, instruct." Pastor, what is God saying to you through your pain? Listen to what He's telling you.

Discipline. He may be disciplining you. Cleaning out some things in your life so you will be more effective for Him. It is better to be pruned to grow than to be cut to burn. The prophet Malachi said the Lord will send the *"refiner's fire"* to *"purify the Levites and refine them like gold and silver."* Seventh Century Christian author Madame Guyon said, "It is the fire of suffering that brings forth the gold of godliness."

Strength. The Lord wants to toughen you through your pain. He has a bigger assignment for you and He is preparing you for it. Through enslavement and imprisonment, God prepared Joseph to be a leader of Egypt and save his people. By caring for his sheep and protecting them from the bear and the lion, David was being prepared to be King of Israel. Bible commentator William Barclay says that a Christian is like an athlete whose spiritual muscles become stronger from the difficulties they face. Sometime back I heard an old proverb which states, "The stronger the breeze the stronger the tree."

Dependence. The Lord may want to simply keep you dependent on Him. Paul had his *"thorn in the flesh."* We each have various thorns that remind us of who we are and keep us focused on the Master. In his book *Failing Forward*, John Maxwell tells the amazing story of Dr. Beck Weathers. Dr. Weathers appeared outwardly very successful. However, there were aspects of his life he knew were not right. While attempting to climb Mount Everest, he had an accident where he lost both of his hands. This tragedy led to a complete reassessment and transformation of his life. He changed from being driven and selfish to being dependent on God and generous. Dr. Weathers said, "Would I like to have my hands back? Sure. Would I like to have my hands back enough to go back to who I was? No."

Intimacy. God always wants your pain to lead to a deeper walk with Him. Through pain, He breaks up the soil of your soul so His roots can go deep into your life. If we respond to pain humbly, it softens us. Pain will loosen us up and break up the hardness in our lives. As we are broken, the Lord is able to plant His roots deeper and deeper into our innermost being. If we allow His roots to penetrate deep into our lives, we will discover heights and enjoy fruitfulness we never imagined possible.

Years ago, I wrote the following in my journal: "You can't experience the true heights of joy until you know the true depths of pain. You can't experience the greatest fruitfulness until you've felt/known the frustration and pain of barrenness."

The Chinese Bamboo tree takes several years to develop an intricate root system while revealing only a small bulb above the ground. Once that root system is established, within one year the tree shoots up dozens of feet in the air.

Doug's Story

As a young father and pastor, Doug Shivers (Boulevard) experienced the most excruciating pain one could ever imagine. I asked Doug to share his story. Here is what he wrote.

> Ten days after our third child was born, my wife Connie, had her first check-up. She had noticed a lump in her chest just below her clavicle. She asked our family physician to look at it. He ordered chest x-rays. A couple of hours after the appointment, we received a call from his office asking us to come back for a follow-up.
>
> Connie had a massive tumor in her chest. I was stunned. I wish I could say I stayed strong, but that day, I fell apart. I sat in a waiting room at the hospital while Connie had a cat-scan, holding our infant daughter, and

wept. A few days later, I asked Connie how she had been so steady, and she informed me, "Well, one of us had to be, you were a mess!"

Connie had Hodgkin's disease, a lymphatic cancer. We were given very optimistic remission and cure rates. Our lives were shaken, but the prospects, while serious, were very hopeful.

The next three years were filled with strange combinations of triumph and despair. We'd receive a great report on her progress, only to have it dashed to pieces in a matter of weeks by another recurrence. She endured chemotherapy, radiation therapy, and a bone marrow transplant. The cancer was relentless. Connie, my wife of 13 years, died Sunday December 15, 1991.

I found myself a single parent of three children ages 10, 7 & 3. I was a pastor. I was 33 years old and had lived through "until death do us part" far earlier than expected.

The pain, during the illness and following her death was overwhelming at times. I struggled to fulfill my duties as husband, father and pastor. My church was very gracious to me. They allowed me to move my study home during the last months of Connie's life. Other moms in the church took turns looking after the children so I could have 2 or 3 days each week to work uninterrupted.

So, what did I learn from the experience?

First, some emotional pain is so great that it overwhelms all self-control. That's not a failure of character; rather it's a humbling reminder of my own limitations.

Second, the Lord's providence is not designed as some kind of message to address particular sins or failures. Of course, the Lord does chasten us, but I never disciplined my own children without their knowing why. My Father is much more righteous and compassionate than I. I cannot imagine Him chastening and then leaving me to figure out what "sin" had provoked the chastening. Suffering may not be for any particular sin or character flaw. Suffering may merely be the purpose of God in your life at that time. I'm often reminded of Job. His suffering wasn't for some sin he'd committed, but was the result of God's own purposes.

Third, always be honest with God about your pain. After all, it's not like you're going to surprise Him by admitting what you're feeling. I found the Psalms to be very helpful in expressing this pain.

Fourth, God is faithful even when I'm nearly faithless. During the end of Connie's illness and for some time after her death, I didn't want to go to church and preach. I did so, a number of times, not because of anything noble, but rather, because it was what was expected of me. It was my job. I can still recall feeling spiritually bereft and entirely alone. Then, I'd begin to preach, and it was as though the Lord opened a "window" from heaven. For a while, the pain was pushed to the background and I was enabled to do what he'd called me to do. I'd finish preaching and before the benediction was over, the "window" was shut, and I was back to the wasteland. The Lord can use me even when I feel the most useless.

Fifth, some things can only be taught by experiencing profound pain. I'm a better pastor because of Connie's illness and death. I'm also a better husband to Laura and father to my children.

Sixth, life in this fallen world is always a life acquainted with suffering and death. We are living in light of another day. The pain I still feel over Connie's death isn't something of which I try to rid myself. It's part of my life in this world. The verse I've held to with all the strength I can summon is Romans 8:18 (ESV):

"For I consider that the sufferings of this present time are not worth comparing with the glory that is to be revealed to us."

Having experienced some of the depths, the greatest of the heights to accomplish this promise fill me with a joyous hope.

Don't Waste Pain

Robert Browning Hamilton said it eloquently in his poem *Along The Road.*

> I walked a mile with pleasure,
> She chattered all the way,
> But left me none the wiser
> For all she had to say.
> I walked a mile with sorrow
> And ne'er a word said she,
> But, Oh, the things I learned from her
> When sorrow walked with me.

C. S. Lewis said, "God whispers to us in our pleasures…but shouts to us in our pain."

God squeezed every bit of good he could from His Son's pain on the cross. There was nothing left. Our sin debt was paid in full. All the grace, love and hope He could gain was squeezed from His pain. What about you? Are you getting full mileage from your pain? Or, is some of the pain in your life wasted? If you are bitter or angry, you are wasting pain. If you are tired or apathetic, you are wasting pain. If you have given up, you are wasting pain. If you are anxious to escape a tough situation, you are wasting pain. If pain doesn't drive you to prayer, you are wasting pain. If pain doesn't drive you to the Bible, you are wasting pain. If pain doesn't drive you to God, you are wasting pain.

If we are not willing to suffer, we will not enjoy the glory. It is an inescapable reality that pain precedes victory. An athlete suffers the pain of practice to gain victory on the field of competition. A woman suffers childbirth to deliver her baby. The Israelites experienced the Wilderness before they possessed the Promised Land. We knew conviction before we enjoyed conversion. Jesus suffered the cross before He celebrated the resurrection.

How strong is our faith? Fourth century Church Father Abbot John the Dwarf challenges us to, "Go and pray to the Lord to command some struggle to be stirred up in you, for the soul is matured only in battles."

During one of Paul's excruciating trials the Lord told him, *"My grace is sufficient for you for my power is made perfect in your weakness."*

Don't waste pain.

Chapter Five

BALANCE

I love to watch the circus performer run around spinning a bunch of plates on sticks all at the same time. As I watch the performer accomplish this feat, I am always relieved when he lifts the plates off the sticks and takes a bow. Once the feat is finished, I feel my body relax and breathe easier. I react this way because spinning a bunch of plates on sticks reminds me of real life.

Who doesn't occasionally feel like the performer trying to keep plates spinning? Who doesn't sometimes feel it takes everything we have just to run from one task to the next and back again, keeping them all propped up and spinning? Many pastors have resigned themselves to believing this is the way life is to be lived. *It is not.*

God did not call us to be "plate spinners." He called us to accomplish His vision and build His Kingdom. He did not call us to run around breathlessly keeping all the programs going and everybody in the church happy. He called us to please Him. To do that, we must live a balanced life.

Living a balanced life is the key to joy, peace and effectiveness. Living a balanced life is not easy in our wild and crazy world. The person (or pastor) who lives a truly balanced life is rare.

How do we live a balanced life? Even though each person must struggle to find their own balance, there are universal principles of balance. Like the performer who follows certain physical principles to spin a bunch of plates at the same time, we must abide by certain God-established principles if we want to live an effective life.

Prioritize Deeply

We hear a lot about priorities. Most of us can rattle off four or five things we call our priorities. If we examine our lives and ministries closely, will we recognize them as true priorities? If not, we have not prioritized deeply enough. For something to be a true priority, we must internalize it. We must think about it, commit to it, and give it the time and energy a true priority deserves.

Is our relationship with the Lord a priority if we spend a minimal amount of time with Him? Is our health a priority if we rarely (if at all) exercise? Is our family a priority if we say "yes" to a myriad of church members' needs, but fail to spend significant time at home? For something (or someone) to be a true priority, we must be willing to say "no" to a multitude of pressing demands because a deeper "yes" (our priority) burns inside us. Writer Robert Louis Stephenson wisely observed, "Perpetual devotion to what man calls his business is only to be sustained by the perpetual neglect of many other things."

Pastor and author John Ortberg wrote a fascinating book, *Overcoming Your Shadow Mission*. He says each of us has a "shadow mission" that will entice us away from our true mission. If not careful, we drift the direction of our "shadow mission" and neglect what we declare to be our actual mission. This temptation to drift is especially a danger for pastors.

Many needs compete for a pastor's attention and energy. For example, we know that the lost are a priority for us. However, few lost people are clamoring to see us so we can bring them to Christ. At the same time, we have a responsibility to care for those from our church who are in the hospital. These members *do* clamor for our attention. If we aren't diligent, we will slip into the "shadow mission" of giving so much time to those in the hospital we don't have anything left for the lost.

The Lord Jesus knew His priorities. He declared, *"For the Son of Man came to seek and save what was lost."* Jesus' priorities were the *cross* and the *lost*. His priorities were internalized so deeply that nothing or no one could distract Him from them. He knew what His life was about. Do we?

I had just started a new pastorate when a young deacon invited me to become a member of his service organization. It sounded like a good idea. The organization met weekly for lunch and performed many worthwhile projects in the community. It offered me an opportunity to meet some people who were outside my normal circle of relationships. I belonged to the organization for only a few months when I realized I had made a mistake. The work involved and time required to be a part of the service organization robbed me of what I knew to be my true priorities. I was living the adage, "The good is the enemy of the best." After I resigned the organization, I felt an overwhelming sense of joy and peace. I knew I had made a decision that would empower me to live my priorities more effectively. We must prioritize deeply.

Relationships

As followers and ministers of Jesus, our relationships must be in order if our life is to be in balance. Jesus taught us relationships are to be primary. He said the first commandment is to love the Lord and the second is to love others as we love ourselves. It doesn't get any clearer than that.

Several years ago, I decided to spend some personal time with an aging grandmother. I knew if I didn't do this quickly, I would soon be standing over her casket regretting missed opportunities. While on a trip to see my grandmother, I realized something. I was driving along thinking about all the undone tasks at church when I was struck with this thought: *Relationships are all that matter*! That was the moment I internalized this priority. I know I had heard, said and probably preached this truth. But at that moment it became mine. It was like a light turned on for me. I knew going to see my grandmother was eternally more important than what needed to be done back at the church.

Jesus gave Himself so the gulf between us and God might be bridged. The crucifixion was (and is) about relationships. We enter the ministry to help people with relationships. First, we want to connect people with God. Second, we want to connect people with others in community (church). As we busy ourselves helping others with their relationships, it is easy for us to neglect our own. It is the proverbial story of the cobbler whose kids have the oldest worn out shoes in town.

Relationships are all that matter. You have heard it said no one on their deathbed is concerned about incomplete programs, undone tasks, or even how many were in Sunday School last Sunday. To live a balanced life, we must know relationships are all that matter.

The Fourth Commandment

We will never live a balanced life if we disobey the Fourth Commandment. Earlier in the book I encouraged you to give your wife a Sabbath. Now I'm going to insist you do the same for yourself. The Sabbath Commandment is about rest. God made us to need rest. Sunday is not a day of rest for pastors. When do you obey the Sabbath Commandment?

What happens if a farmer plants and harvests the same crop on the same plot of land season after season? What happens if a mechanic runs a car twenty-four hours a day seven days a week? What happens if a basketball coach runs his team hour after hour non-stop? Invariably, the soil is depleted and won't produce, the car breaks down and the ball players collapse. Physical laws predetermine soil usage, mechanical failure and physical limits.

What happens if a pastor refuses to take a day off and pushes himself day after day and week after week? It's been said we don't break God's laws—we simply break ourselves against them. The pastor who breaks the Sabbath Commandment suffers the consequences of his own foolishness and disobedience. Here is a partial list of the problems that result from breaking the Fourth

Commandment: spiritual weakness; lack of joy; inability to focus; sleep problems; stress; anger; indecisiveness; forgetfulness; fear; alienation of family; depression; burn-out.

Pastor Mark Buchanan wrote a book about Sabbath keeping and breaking. He said, "The world is not dying for another book. But it is dying for the rest of God. I certainly was. I became a Sabbath–Keeper the hard way: either that, or die." For many pastors, it's too late. They have either opted for a substandard Christian and pastoral life (rocking along in neutral), burned out or are already on the sidelines of ministry.

In *Ordering Your Private World*, Gordon McDonald tells the story of a nineteenth century scientist who was exploring parts of unmapped Africa. He hired a group of native men to be his guides and provide support for the trip. The first three days of the exploration they made very good time and were ahead of schedule. The explorer was thrilled. On the fourth day, the explorer awakened expecting the natives to be moving around breaking camp. However, the camp was quiet. When he asked what was going on, he was told the natives would be taking the day off. Since they had made such good time, they needed to stop and *"let their souls catch up with their bodies."*

Obeying the Fourth Commandment is not rocket science. It states, *"Six days you shall labor…but the seventh day is a Sabbath to the Lord…on it you shall not do any work."* Pastors must find a day (or more) each week to relax, not work, have fun, get out of their normal routine and recharge their batteries. That is a law. If we break it, we suffer. If we obey it, we win and the Kingdom wins.

Margin

Margin means we take the principle of the Sabbath and apply it to every area of our lives. Have you ever tried to read a page with no margin? A page that is single-spaced, top to bottom and edge to edge. It is frustrating, hard work and boring. It is what our lives are like when we live without margin. Doctor, missionary and author Richard Swenson says the disease of our culture is "marginless living."

The world is changing at breakneck speed. I was visiting with my mother-in-law recently about this. She told me that growing up her family didn't have electricity until she was a teenager. Now she carries her cell phone with her wherever she goes, e-mails her grandkids daily and won't drive out of her driveway unless her GPS is up and running.

In the last century we have gone from *some* change to *occasional* change to *rapid* change to *exponential* change. Consider the change in the amount of knowledge that is accumulating today. We have moved from adding to the knowledge we have in the world to doubling it. Then doubling it again. And then doubling it again and again and again. Knowledge is accumulating so rapidly that no person, library or computer can keep up with it. Dr. Swenson tells the following story in his book *Margin*. A graduate class of business students was given the following question: If you folded a piece of paper in half forty times, how thick would it be? Most of the students thought it would be less than one foot. Some said it would be greater that one mile. How thick do you think it would be? The answer is: the stack of paper would be thick enough to extend from the earth to the moon.

Change is happening so rapidly that no one can keep up with even a fraction of it. Yet, we allow changes and technological advances to slowly (or rapidly) take over our lives and squeeze out any breathing room we may have left. The margin in our lives get smaller and smaller. White space darkens. Gaps are filled up.

Who controls the spaces or margin in your life? Who determines what happens between the lines and around the edges of your life? Do you allow others to take over the spaces and edges of your life or do you protect those for yourself. Several years ago there was a fascinating court case regarding ownership of spaces. Radio stations were taking Rush Limbaugh's daily radio talk show and altering it to their advantage. Rush has very distinct pauses or spaces when he talks. Radio stations were taking his recordings and speeding up his program by squeezing the pauses or spaces between words. This allowed them to squeeze in more advertisements. Rush sued the stations and won. His contention was that he owned his words and the spaces between them.

Dr. Swenson says, "Margin…is having breath left at the top of the staircase, money left at the end of the month and sanity left at the end of adolescence…margin is energy…margin is security." Our fast paced culture says we must stay constantly busy doing, going, working, keeping up and trying harder or we will lose this thing called life. Culture is wrong. We must fight back. We must reclaim some margin in our lives. Dr. Swenson lists several prescriptions to help us reclaim margin. They are: cultivate social support; reconcile relationships; serve one another; rest; laugh; cry; create appropriate boundaries; grant grace; and above all, love.

Plan Weekly

One of the main reasons we have trouble living our priorities, leaving margin in our lives and living in balance is the way we do planning. Pastors need to do weekly (or longer) planning. Many pastors are still stuck in daily planning. What do I mean? Instead of waiting until the beginning of each day to decide the focus and schedule for the day, take time at the beginning of each week to plan the week. Sit down, look over the week and go ahead and schedule your sermon preparation time, outreach, hospital visitation, exercise routine and family time. In other words, be intentional and proactive regarding your schedule. You need to write it down or put it in your electronic planner. Don't drift through each day reacting to whatever presses against you the hardest. Don't allow your shadow mission to creep in and take over. Be responsible for your life. Plan ahead.

I had a well-meaning seminary professor who said the pastorate is a "life of interruptions." It is true that our calling assumes a certain level of availability. But if we live our lives based on interruptions, we will never accomplish our true priorities. If we schedule things we can control, it is amazing how other things will either fall by the wayside (and not need our attention after all) or wait until we are available. In *First Things First*, Stephen Covey says, "The key...is not to prioritize your schedule, but to schedule your priorities." You know what your life is about. Live it!

Recreation and Laughter

Fun and recreation are imperative for balance. The first several years of our marriage Robbi and I didn't have enough money or time to take much of a vacation. We would spend whatever little vacation time we had mooching off our parents. I believe it was in the tenth year of our marriage and the summer following our fifth year in our first pastorate that we scraped together enough money to buy some used camping equipment at a garage sale. With our garage sale camping equipment and a spirit of adventure, the four of us went on our first real family vacation. We camped in Tennessee and Arkansas and had a blast. After that first successful vacation, we decided we would do whatever it took to save money and set aside the time to go on an honest-to-goodness two week vacation to the beach the next year.

We did it. We borrowed a small camper and spent nearly two weeks on South Padre Island, Texas. I vividly remember sitting at a picnic table beside the camper cleaning seashells and thinking about how relaxed and energized I was. When we returned from that vacation I had more energy and enthusiasm for ministry than at any time since I began pastoring. This experience sold me on the need for recreation.

Recreation means to create anew or re-create. It means to be refreshed, reinvigorated, reenergized and be re-born. We know the fun and enthusiasm of creation.

When my first grandbaby, Molly Cate, was born (created), it was exhilarating. Every grandparent understands that feeling. I remember the first time she smiled at me and said, "Granddaddy." Actually, it was more like "Ga-ran-datty." I loved it. It was fun. It was a new thing she did. It was a fresh creation. And I was re-created!

What is recreation for you? What re-creates you? We are blessed to have many pastors in our Association who understand this need and who practice healthy re-creation. Here are a few examples.

Don Washam (Sycamore) plays golf, Mitch Fisher (Center) goes fishing, Daryl Walker (Clear Creek) rides his motorcycle, John Justice (Homeland) listens to rock-n-roll music from the 1960's and Lex Fox (Pleasant Home) plays his guitar with his old music buddies.

Lex can play and sing every Beatles' song ever recorded. On a mission trip to Guadalajara, Mexico, a Mexican pastor found out about Lex's talent and insisted he lead some Mexican pastors in old Beatles' tunes. It was hilarious.

When is the last time you laughed so hard you cried? When is the last time you laughed so hard you lost control and had to sit down or you would have fallen down? Medical research tells us laughter reduces stress and lowers blood pressure. Abraham Lincoln kept a book of jokes in his desk drawer at the White House. He would regularly take out the book read a joke and laugh. On one occasion he told his cabinet, "If I couldn't laugh, I would die."

Isn't life fun? Recreation and laughter are necessary for balance. Are you having enough fun in your life?

The Goose and The Golden Eggs

One of Aesop's ancient fables illustrates the need for a balanced life.

One morning a poor farmer checked beneath his goose for an egg. He found what appeared to be an egg, but when he picked it up he realized it was too heavy to be an egg. He thought someone must be trying to trick him and so he decided to throw it away. But on second thought he decided he would take it to town and find out what it was. To his amazement and delight, he discovered it was solid gold. The next morning he hurried out to check the goose and discovered another golden egg. He couldn't believe his good fortune. This continued for some time until the farmer became very rich. However, the more wealth he accumulated the more impatient he became. Finally, he became so impatient he picked up the goose, killed it and cut it open expecting to find it full of golden eggs. Of course, there were none.

We (pastors) are the goose. How many times have we tried to produce more and more golden eggs only to wear ourselves out and kill the goose? Balance is the way we both produce golden eggs and keep the goose healthy enough to produce more golden eggs.

Constant Adjustments

When an airplane takes off it has a flight plan mapped out to get to its destination. I've been told that an airplane is slightly off its flight plan ninety percent of the time. That means the pilot must constantly be making adjustments to get the plane back on track. Most of the time we are off line in our plan to live a balanced life. But if we live according to God's principles and if we make regular adjustments, we will achieve the joy, peace and effectiveness we want.

Stop running around spinning plates. Live with balance.

Chapter Six

WHAT'S A PASTOR TO DO?
(Don't Resign – Until It's Time)

It was late on a Sunday night when the phone rang. With a quivering, tear-filled voice, a pastor in our Association blurted out, "Mike, I broke my promise to you." This pastor was under a great deal of stress in his church. There was growing opposition to his ministry. I made him promise he wouldn't resign without first talking to me. During a heated Deacon's meeting, he became angry, felt cornered and suddenly resigned. He broke his promise.

Not long ago, a pastor in our Association stood in his pulpit on a Sunday morning and, seemingly out of the clear blue, resigned. He was not going to another church nor did he have another job. Church members were shocked over the resignation. Truthfully, it had been building inside this pastor for some time. He later told me, "I'm burned out." He also confessed that he was literally driving to see me on a couple of occasions to talk about his struggles and each time he was distracted by ministry responsibilities.

What's a pastor to do? Both of these pastors are good guys who had fruitful ministries in their churches. Is there anything a pastor can do to avoid the pain, frustration and tragedy these pastors experienced? Or, are we simply victims of immature church members, unbiblical expectations, criticism and any problems or crises that arise in the church? Are our only recourses to resign, be fired or collapse? Absolutely not! We are in control of our lives. We control our thoughts, decisions and actions. There are several things we can do—and we must do—if we are to survive and thrive as pastors. We are children of the King. We have a unique and vital calling. We have an Advocate in the Holy Spirit who is with us at all times. It doesn't matter how dire the situation becomes, there are always steps we can take.

Self Care

Remember, as pastor, *you* are the *most important* **human resource** God gives your church. You are more important than any other resource except the Bible and the Holy Spirit. Since you are the church's most important *human resource*, it makes sense you would do regular maintenance.

Our Association is blessed to have an outstanding Disaster Relief Ministry Chain Saw Unit. What would happen if our Chain Saw Team was so busy cutting limbs and trees and cleaning up after disasters they never took time to sharpen the blades on their saws? Over time, the saws would get dull, not cut and be useless. At that point, the Chain Saw Unit would become ineffective and probably cease to exist. How many pastors have resigned or been forced out simply because they didn't sharpen the saw? In *The 7 Habits of Highly Effective People*, Stephen Covey says to "sharpen the saw" is a "Principle of Balanced Self-Renewal."

In previous chapters I've written about the need to take care of ourselves. I particularly addressed our responsibility to care for ourselves spiritually, care for our family, manage our schedule, keep the Sabbath and have fun. Here are three more ways we need to practice self-care.

Physically. Many pastors are a mess physically: over-weight; high blood pressure; high cholesterol; sinus problems; neck and back pain and other problems. We know what we need to do, but we don't do it. We need to love and respect ourselves enough to get in better physical shape. This is vital if we are to be in control of our lives. When we don't take care of ourselves physically it has a multiplying effect that drags down every other part of our lives.

Few of us will do what the following pastors have done. Denny Marr (Calvary) has run a 10k in under 40 minutes. Tony

Turner (NorthBridge) is a martial–arts instructor and a 3rd degree black belt in Kenpo Karate. Chad Killingsworth (Emmaus) hiked the Appalachian Trail (2150 miles in 5 months) and the Pacific Crest Trail that goes from Mexico to Canada. Nolan Carrier (South Gate) biked the 270 mile Katy Trail numerous times. But, each of us can get in better shape. I can't tell you what to do, but I can give you a kick in the pants to help you get started.

Here's what I do. Robbi and I walk two miles several times a week. I go to the gym three times a week and lift weights, stretch and strengthen my core. I always feel better when I leave the gym. I'm in much better shape than I was several years ago, but still have a lot of room for improvement.

Another way we need to take care of ourselves physically is to faithfully go to the doctor and dentist for check-ups. Pastor, when is the last time you had a physical exam? When is the last time you had blood work done? What is your cholesterol? What is your PSA? What is your blood pressure? If you are over fifty, have you had a colonoscopy? Our bodies are the means by which we live our lives, love our families, have fun and conduct our ministries. If our bodies decline, it impacts every part of our lives including our effectiveness as pastors. Take care of your body. You will live longer, live better and be a more effective pastor.

Mentally. What do you do to stay sharp mentally? Please don't tell me your plan for mental development includes reading all the e-mail forwards you receive while either listening to BASS COUNTRY (92.9 FM) or Rush Limbaugh. Actually, I read some of my e-mail forwards, love BASS COUNTRY and occasionally (rarely) listen to Rush. But, these things do nothing to grow and sharpen me mentally.

It is easy for pastors to get lazy mentally. This hit me recently when both my eighty year old Dad and thirty-three year old son beat me in chess on the same day. I used to be a pretty good chess player, but after the humiliation of those losses I thought, "Mike, your mind is squishy."

While we were in college and seminary, we were accountable to read, study, debate, present papers and do other things that kept our minds working and growing. Since then, it is easy to fall into routines (ruts) and get so busy with ministry our minds atrophy. We may prepare Bible studies and sermons, but we don't present fresh and challenging material. Over time it is the same old stuff. If we aren't careful, we begin to rely on other preachers and selected websites for most of our sermon ideas and outlines.

Pastor, how much do you read? Reading is for the mind what exercise is for the body. You need to read the newspaper, magazines and books. You need to read novels, theology, biographies, science, leadership, management, church health, history, Christian discipleship, commentaries, personal growth, family development, psychology and other kinds of books. Reading stretches your mind and keeps you fresh. It keeps you in touch with culture and your people. It gives you an inexhaustible supply of sermon material.

The pastor who doesn't read, or who only reads material with which he already agrees, is doomed to irrelevance. Many pastors only (or primarily) read material by pastors or church leaders who are just like them. They read authors who believe like them, think like them and act like them. When is the last time you read a book that really challenged you? A book that stretched you to think about things that made you uncomfortable?

I recently read Frank Schaeffer's book *Crazy For God*. Frank Schaeffer is Francis and Edith Schaeffer's son. Frank directed the two video series' *How Should We Then Live?* and *Whatever Happened to the Human Race?* He became a leader in the conservative Christian movement of the 1980's. He was a key-note speaker at the Southern Baptist Convention. He was heard several times on James Dobson's *Focus on the Family* radio program, Pat Robertson's *700 Club* and from Jerry Falwell's pulpit. He was in demand throughout the country as a preacher and Christian spokesman. Along with his father, he was at the forefront of the anti-abortion movement. The sub-title of his book is, *How I Grew Up As One Of The Elect, Helped Found The Religious Right, And Lived To Take All (Or Most All) Of It Back.*

Today Frank Schaeffer belongs to a Greek Orthodox Church and questions everything about his former faith. I read this book knowing full well it would challenge me. It not only challenged me, it disturbed me. But I'm glad I read it. I am stronger mentally and spiritually for it.

Longshoreman and philosopher Eric Hoffer said, "In times of change, the learners will inherit the Earth, while the knowers will find themselves beautifully equipped to deal with a world that no longer exists."

Never stop learning. Never stop reading. Your church and the Kingdom depend on it.

Socially. Pastors and their wives need friends. Earlier in the book I wrote about my need for solitude. I need social interaction as well. If I don't have regular interaction with good friends, I feel disconnected, frustrated and depressed.

Pastors are lonely. Even though pastors serve in the midst of people it is easy to feel isolated. The fact is most of our church relationships take more than they give. If all (or most) of our relationships take more than they give, over time there is nothing left of us. We need to develop friendships with people who give us as much as we give them. We need people in our lives who encourage us, listen to us and love us for *who we are* and not *what we do*. People who will come to our aid at any moment. Friends who will help us laugh. Friends who will help us cry. Friends who will be at our bedside when we die.

Developing this depth of friendship takes work. We have to find people with whom we want to develop this depth of relationship and then break through the typical superficial level of relationship we have with church members, neighbors and others.

Can pastors and their wives have close friends in their church? When I first entered the pastorate I was told by several pastors and denominational leaders I shouldn't develop close friendships with church members. I understood the warning. Wise pastors will be cautious about forming close friendships with church members. However, Robbi and I have found a pastor and family can form very meaningful and life-long friendships with selected church members. Obviously, a pastor can't have that level of friendship with many in the church.

While pastoring in Harrisonville, Missouri, Robbi and I became dear friends with Laurence and Renee Smith. Laurence and Renee are business owners. They were leaders in our church. Our kids are about the same age. We have similar interests. Robbi and Renee love interior decorating and travel. Laurence and I love to fish. During our time in Harrisonville, we grew close. That relationship continues today. Our relationship is interdependent and mutually beneficial. We talk about everything. When I'm with Laurence I am relaxed. He knows me well and accepts me for who I am. After our time together, I am encouraged and feel stronger and better. Laurence has been with me on two mission trips to India. And so, yes, a pastor and wife can have dear friends who are members of their church. But be careful. Sometimes seemingly high level friendships with church members will backfire.

Whether or not you develop close friends within the church, every pastor and wife need close friends outside the church. Since pastors eat, sleep, and breathe church, they need social interaction with people they love and trust who are not closely connected to their church. They need friends who don't know the church issues, problems or the problem people in the church. Pastor, do you and your wife have some of those kinds of friends? You need them. You need good friends.

Grace Yourself

We are in the Jesus business. Jesus is about grace. John wrote, *"The Word became flesh and made his dwelling among us. We have seen his glory, the glory of the One and Only, who came from the Father, full of grace and truth…From the fullness of his grace we have all received one blessing after another."* As followers of Jesus, we are to be filled with grace. We are to live lives in light of God's grace. We are to extend His grace to others. And we are to grace ourselves.

Pastors are good at accepting and enjoying the grace of God in their lives. They faithfully acknowledge and thank God for his grace. Pastors love to sing of God's grace. One of my favorite Hymns is *Wonderful Grace of Jesus*. Following is the first verse and chorus of that beautiful Hymn.

Wonderful grace of Jesus, Greater than all my sin;
How shall my tongue describe it, Where shall its praise begin?
Taking away my burden, Setting my spirit free,
For the wonderful grace of Jesus reaches me.

Wonderful the matchless grace of Jesus
Deeper than the mighty rolling sea
Higher than the mountain, sparkling like a fountain
All sufficient grace for even me.
Broader than the scope of my transgressions,
Greater far than all my sin and shame;
O magnify the precious name of Jesus,
Praise His name!

Pastors are also good at extending grace to others. From the pulpit, they talk openly about the love and forgiveness of God. Through tears, they plead with people to give themselves to God and experience His grace. When people come to their pastor for counseling he will inevitably emphasize God's grace. He urges those he's counseling to accept God's grace and forgiveness and forgive themselves.

Pastors are good at forgiving and forgetting when church members fail. If a church leader fails at a task, pastors are quick to extend grace. If a staff member makes a mistake, pastors overlook it and just keep on going. Pastors enjoy dispensing grace to others. It is a part of their call and ministry. It is a result of the grace they themselves have experienced from God.

But pastors are *not* good at giving grace to themselves. Why? Why are we good at extending grace to others, but bad at giving grace to ourselves? We readily forgive and forget the failures, sins and mistakes of church members, but we beat ourselves up over and over again for the slightest error. Why? It has to do with the unbiblical and unrealistic expectations that others place on us and that we place on ourselves. We assume (or know) people are watching us. We're afraid mistakes or failures will be devastating to others and the church. We are such people pleasers we don't want to do anything that someone (especially a church member) might criticize or hold against us.

It goes back to whether we are primarily *human beings* or *human doings*. With those kinds of expectations and that kind of pressure, it's a struggle to simply be a *human being*. We know better, but it seems we can't help it. We think of ourselves as some super-human creation. We place ourselves on a higher level than the average run-of-the-mill church member. Honestly, we do have a serious responsibility that requires our best. If we fail, people may be hurt. But we are still human beings. God made us human—not super-human. We need to accept our humanity, enjoy our humanity and extend the same grace to ourselves that we receive from God and give to others.

Pastor, you need to relax, breathe deeply and smile. As you receive the wonderful grace of God, you need to grace yourself. Allow yourself to be a real-life flesh and blood human being. Thank God for who you are and the life He has given you. This is the gift of grace.

Confront

Several years ago Pastor Stephen Brown wrote an article for *Leadership* magazine entitled, *Developing a Christian Mean Streak.* He tells the story of the time a Pastor Search Committee asked him to come to their church. He questioned why they were interested in him. The committee told him they had a fellow in their church that gave lots of money and pushed everyone around. The three previous pastors left because of him. People were afraid of him. No one in the church was willing to confront him. The church needed a pastor who was mean enough to handle the guy. The committee told Brown they thought he was their man because he had a reputation for being tough. Brown told the committee they didn't need a pastor. They needed a drill sergeant. In the article he explained that pastors need to know how to appropriately confront people if they are to have a healthy church. He said, "All too often in American churches, pastors are sitting ducks for neurotic church members."

Confrontation is difficult for most pastors. None of us go into this business to confront people. We go into ministry to love, serve and bless people. However, every pastor knows you must be able to look situations and people in the eye and confront them. If a pastor can't do that, he will suffer and his church will suffer.

Jesus knew when and how to confront people. He confronted the sellers and money changers in the Temple. He confronted Nicodemus when he said, *"You must be born again."* Jesus confronted Peter about his betrayal. He confronted the religious establishment over their traditions. He confronted Pilate with His silence. He confronts all of us with His crucifixion and resurrection.

Jesus instructs us to confront. He says, *"If your brother sins against you, go and show him his fault, just between the two of you."* The passage goes on to explain that if the brother won't listen to us, we need to take someone else and confront him again. If that doesn't work, we take it before the church.

We let problems fester too long. We don't need to jump into every issue or criticism that surfaces in the church. But, if a problem persists or is serious it must be dealt with. If problem people continue stirring up difficulties, they need to be addressed.

I heard Baptist leader Jimmy Draper say, "If someone slings mud on you and you try to brush it off immediately, it just smears. But, if you wait a little while the mud will dry and it brushes off easily." I agree. But if someone keeps slinging mud on you, they must be confronted.

I let a problem in one of my churches go too far. A deacon in the church was very critical of me, our Youth Minister and the church's youth ministry. I tried to ignore him and his criticisms. Our youth ministry was reaching many teenagers for Christ by using innovative and progressive methods. This deacon felt we were compromising with the world by using some of these methods.

One evening we conducted a large regional youth event in our Fellowship Hall. Several hundred teenagers were in attendance. A Christian youth band was going to town with loud and lively music. Adult sponsors were serving pizza and Cokes. The place was buzzing. This deacon showed up at the event uninvited. His sole purpose was to spy and find fault. After walking around, listening and watching, he approached me and was very angry. He got right up in my face and screamed, ***"That's rock music in the church."*** He then put his hands on my chest and shoved me against a wall. I came off the wall in a rage. I vividly remember telling myself, "Mike, keep your hands at your side." I desperately wanted to slug him right between the eyes. I then very calmly but directly told him to leave. He left immediately. Several days later we met. He apologized for his behavior. I accepted his apology. I then told him he was not going to be happy in our church or with my leadership. I said it was time for him and his family to leave our church. Soon after that, they left.

There are bullies in our churches. Almost every church has someone (or several) who take it on themselves to criticize, gossip about, undercut and otherwise beat up their pastor. We must be ready and willing to take on these people. We shouldn't be reactive, but we must be deliberate. We need to think and pray through the appropriate way to confront these bullies and then take steps to do it.

To begin with, we need to involve other leaders in the process. Pastors are reluctant to tell others in the church about difficult people. That is a mistake. If a problem person is causing us or the church serious problems, we need to inform and involve other church leaders. Even if we are the one who will do the confronting we need to make sure others know what is going on. Mature church leaders want to know—and need to know—about problems that negatively impact their church and their pastor. People who need to be confronted are not solely a pastor issue, but a church issue as well. Remember, as pastor, you are the *most important human resource* your church has. Your people need to know when their most important human resource hurts or is under attack. We need to let the body be aware of the problems in the body so the body can heal itself.

I learned valuable lessons through the incident with the deacon. First, I learned not to let problems build to the point of explosion. Second, I learned that when I stood up to confront a difficult person I had lots of support. Church leaders were simply waiting for me to take a firm stand. Third, I learned that when people knew I was willing to confront problem people some of the problems and criticisms in the church quietly disappeared. Finally, I was reminded we are always in the midst of spiritual warfare. When God moves (as He was doing in our youth ministry) the enemy will pull out the stops to squelch it.

Don't develop a "mean streak." Do learn how to appropriately confront problem people. Be courageous.

Buddies

Webster's New International Dictionary defines a buddy as, "companion, partner, fellow soldier and intimate friend." Pastors need buddies. We need fellow pastors and ministers with whom we can share our lives. A men's Bible study group in the church is good. But we (as pastors) can't be fully transparent in that type of group. We need a group of peers. Men who know and understand our struggles, stress and burdens. Men who will love us, hold us accountable and stand with us in tough times.

Nolan Carrier (South Gate) was instrumental in organizing a group of ministers who meet regularly. I asked Nolan to share some thoughts about the importance of buddies.

Nolan's Experience

There was a time in my ministry when I was so very, very connected. Connected with other pastors and church leaders. I went to conventions. I served on boards. In those settings there was always time to catch up and share with trusted friends the joys, pain, struggles and challenges of vocational ministry. It was the primary reason to stay involved in those events. Then twelve years ago, or so, the winds of change blew hard over Missouri Baptist life and there was no appeal to attend conventions and meetings. I did not miss those gatherings but I did miss the connection with trusted friends. That void continued to grow. Then I decided, to survive, I had to take some initiative to get reconnected with sojourners on a deeper level.

God brought a group of men into my life that recognized the same need in their lives. So we signed up. We made a commitment to spend about 50 hours a year together. We would share from deep inside ourselves. We would do a quick analysis of each other at our gatherings and determine who was carrying the heaviest load and focus on that person until there were no sloping shoulders, no more tears and no more, or at least fewer, wrinkles in their face. We strive to put spring in each other's steps, joy in hearts and hope in our souls. We strive to be transparent. We admit mistakes and sin knowing that healing and strength comes when we are honest with ourselves, with each other and with God. We believe in Proverbs 27:17, "As iron sharpens iron, so one man sharpens another." We strive to be a Jonathan to a David and David to a Jonathan. We are committed to each other through "thick and sin." Yes, I said it the way I intended to. No man is an island. When I act like an island I get into trouble. There are more sins, more me and less of God. My buddies pray for me, encourage me, love me, yes, even me. They give me a hard time. You do that with people you love and are comfortable with.

If these buddies had not come along, there is a big, big possibility that I would not be in vocational ministry today. That is the measure of impact they have had on my life. They have been a lifeline. God has used them to pull me up and put me on solid ground. I would say a full time vocational minister would be foolish not to be so connected.

Power of Group

Nolan's testimony is evidence of the power of a group of buddies getting together for mutual good. I've seen that power transform men from being on the edge of resigning their church and leaving the ministry to renewal and effective ministry. It's amazing what happens to us when we trust selected friends and allow their grace to heal and empower us.

Many years ago I participated in a leadership laboratory training experience for ministers. During this training, I witnessed the overwhelming power of a group. This leadership training experience involved forming small groups of ministers that jointly worked on projects and faced challenges together. It involved getting to know others in your group at a high level of intimacy. It involved developing strong trust to work on stressful projects. One fellow in my group was named Bob. He was a pastor in north Missouri. This experience was so profound I recorded some of it in my journal.

The greatest experience of the entire week for me was watching Bob experience the most dramatic change I've ever seen in a person in that length of time. Bob has experienced every kind of heartache imaginable. Rejection of parents, failure, divorce, ministry problems, child attempted suicide, teenage daughter pregnant. Bob has been in intensive counseling for 10 months. He has a terrible self-image. At the beginning of the week he was a terrified little boy. His face ashen, his hair disheveled, his leg bouncing from nervousness. At the end of the week he would look you straight in the eye (something he said he'd never been able to do), his face relaxed (handsome), his smile confident, and his body relaxed. It was a miracle. It was the result of the affirming, loving grace of God passing though a group of men to a hurting brother. The acceptance and love we poured out on him caused (forced, encouraged) him to see how special Bob is and begin to accept himself.

I remember an experience with Bob I didn't record in my journal. One evening the group went out for pizza. We had a blast just telling stories, laughing and being together. At the end of the evening, Bob told the guys that as far as he could remember, it was the first time in his life he had ever been out for an evening with the guys (buddies). I could have cried. I thought, "How many pastors are out there entirely on their own. No buddies to go out with and laugh and tell stories and cut-up."

I still cry when I think there may be pastors in our Association like Bob. It doesn't have to be like that. We've got several groups of pastors that meet regularly. If you are out there alone, stop it! Get with one of these groups or form your own group. You need buddies!

Be Tough

Pastors must be tough. The work of pastoring a local church is not for the faint-of-heart. There are times in the ministry when a pastor simply has to grit his teeth, focus on the future and keep putting one foot in front of the other.

I remember Sundays when I didn't know if I would make it. While driving to church on those Sundays, I remember thinking, "I'm empty. I don't have anything to give. How am I going to preach, conduct meetings and give myself to people today?" And then I prayed, "Lord, I'm weak and empty. I need Your strength and Your spirit to empower and use me." Somehow, by the power and grace of God, I made it. Sometimes, something good would happen on those days. When that happened I smiled and thanked God. I took it as His way of reminding me it's not about me, but about Him. Have you ever had those kinds of days? Days when you had nothing left to give? Days when you felt used up? I know you have. Every pastor has those days.

George Washington said, "Perseverance and spirit have done wonders in all ages." To survive and thrive, pastors must be tough and resilient.

We are forever grateful the Lord Jesus was tough. At His darkest moment He cried out, *"Father, if you are willing, take this cup from me…"* He was close to throwing in the towel. The responsibility and weight were overwhelming. The fear was debilitating. It was the hinge-point of history. It could have gone either way. But the Lord was tough. He completed His prayer with, *"…yet not my will, but yours be done."* He fulfilled His calling.

Each of us has been through extremely difficult times. That goes with the territory of being a pastor. Each of us has thought about quitting. Each of us has reached a point where we didn't think we could go on. What do we do if we reach that point? One thing we can do is remember the distance between "hard" and "can't do it anymore" is great. It is a long way from "tough" to "quit." Let me explain.

I lift weights at the gym three days a week. One exercise I'm currently doing is the dumbbell incline press. This exercise involves my sitting on a bench with the back of the bench at a forty-five degree angle. I take a thirty pound dumbbell in each hand, lean back on the bench, put the weights on each side of my head and then press them over-head. As I do this exercise, it gets hard on about the fifth repetition. However, at that point I'm just getting started. If I quit as soon as it gets tough, I wouldn't work hard enough for the exercise to do me much good. I'm not finished with the exercise until I've done three sets of fifteen repetitions each. Sometimes on the final set I push myself to the limit of maybe eighteen or twenty reps. At that point, I'm sweating, breathing hard, straining and my arms are shaking with exhaustion. So, the distance between "hard" and "can't do it any more" is much greater than you think.

Pastor, you are stronger than you think you are. The enemy likes to bluff you into believing you are at the end of your rope when you actually have a lot of rope left. Poker is a good game for pastors to play (without gambling real money!). In poker you learn to look for the bluff. You learn to judge whether your opponent really has the cards to beat you or whether he is bluffing to get you to quit. Our enemy, Satan, is a deceiver and bluffer. He knows just which strings to pull to bluff us into thinking we have no option but to resign. He convinces us that just because it is hard, we can't do it anymore. And we fall for it. We fold when we don't have to. We quit even though we're holding good cards in our hand.

A dear friend of mine was pastor of a large church in the Kansas City area. The enemy worked his bluff on my friend and he became convinced that people in the church wanted him to leave. One Sunday night, at the close of his sermon, he suddenly resigned and walked out of the building. Fortunately, the church had mature leaders who knew their pastor made a mistake. The church refused his resignation. Instead, they gave him a sabbatical. Two months later he returned with an entirely different perspective. He was renewed and re-energized. My friend continued to pastor the church for several more very successful years.

The systems in the ocean work just as much during low tide as high tide. They work just as much between waves as during a large wave. In fact, between waves (ebb) the ocean is gathering strength and energy for the wave (flow). Oftentimes, pastors get discouraged and quit during the ebb times. They fail to recognize that the Lord is just as powerfully at work as always. In fact, He may be using the ebb time to prepare the church for a big wave. If the pastor quits, he under-cuts the Lord's plans and misses the next big wave.

Pastor, you are stronger than you think. It may be hard, but that is a long way from quitting. Be tough!

Gary Merkel (Harmony) was on the verge of quitting. He felt he failed his church and didn't know what else to do. I asked Gary to share his story.

Gary's Story

At times in ministry it is possible to feel like quitting or moving on. I was there several years ago. After sixteen years of very fruitful ministry and an incredible start on my new field, my heart was crushed over a business meeting where our congregation was split. I had never had it happen before and I felt I had totally failed my church family. I felt that a "power struggle" was going to end what started so beautifully. I sought counsel from Mike Haynes and he helped me think and pray through the situation. Through persevering prayer and laying aside hurts God healed and the ministry has blossomed. Had I left prematurely, I believe it would have been devastating for the church and for me. What my church family and I saw was the grace of God at work. Pushing through the difficulty and depending on God has led to the building of a new worship center, a growing church, sending out a missionary from our church to Guatemala and sending out more than 100 volunteer missionaries from our church over the last three years. I am truly blessed as I complete my seventh year at Harmony.

Don't Resign

Don't resign—until it's time. There is an appropriate time to resign. There are legitimate reasons to resign. Pastors need to do everything in their power to resign at the right time, for the right reasons and on their terms.

Most pastor resignations happen for positive reasons. The pastor is moving to another church, taking another ministry position, retiring or making a change for other appropriate purposes. I encourage pastors who leave under these kinds of circumstances to do everything possible to finish well. Give your family and the church enough time to say a healthy "goodbye." Don't resign and be gone within just a couple of weeks. That leaves a bad taste in everyone's mouth. Refuse the temptation to take one final shot at people in the church who didn't support your ministry or caused you problems. How you finish at one church will have a lot to do with how you begin at another church.

Even though most pastor resignations are positive, many are not. A growing number of pastors are resigning out of stress, frustration, anger, fear or other illegitimate reasons. This type of resignation is devastating to the pastor and his family and causes long-term problems in the church.

If a pastor is tempted to resign due to his own stress and frustration, he needs to do the following.

First, he must *objectively assess* the situation. If possible, he should take a few days vacation, go on a personal retreat or attend a helpful seminar or conference. He needs to get away from the stress of the church and its constant demands so he can take a more thoughtful look at his situation. If it is not possible to get away for a few vacation or renewal days, he should simply take a few medical "stress" days to gather himself and reflect on the situation.

Second, he needs *counsel*. When we are in the midst of a high stress situation and contemplating a major life change we need advice. Sometimes our view is so myopic we can't trust our perspective. We need someone (friend or counselor) who can help us be objective and see the big picture.

Third, if a pastor continues to feel it is time to resign, he needs to *line up another church, ministry position or job* before actually resigning. Pastors are overly optimistic about getting another church or job right away. I hear from pastors all over the country who resigned their churches thinking they could jump into another pastorate within a few weeks or months. That rarely happens.

Finally, whatever the circumstances, he needs to *resign in as positive and generous a way as possible*. A pastor needs to leave his church with a spirit of grace and thanksgiving. Remember how the Lord Jesus did it while He was on the cross. The pastor doesn't want to say or do anything that would empower or justify his opposition and hurt or weaken his friends.

Now, what does a pastor do if he is being pressured to resign? Again, the first thing he needs to do is get a healthy perspective. Is this pressure from just a few individual detractors or is it from a significant power base or group? After taking the necessary time off and receiving counseling, he may need to talk directly to key leaders in the church. The pastor needs to discover the truth about the breadth and depth of the opposition to his ministry. I have counseled several pastors who thought they were on the verge of losing their church only to discover their detractors were few and far between. They actually had strong support in the church.

My Granddad Dondee was a big Yankees fan. He used to tell me lots of stories about Babe Ruth and all the great Yankee players. He told me this story. Casey Stengel, the long-time manager of the New York Yankees, was asked how he remained manager of the Yankees for so many years. He said, "The key is to keep the guy that hates you from getting together with the guy who hasn't made up his mind yet." Well, I'm not sure that would work in the pastorate. It seems like those folks always have a way of getting together, whatever we do to keep them apart.

Another thing to remember is the church calls the pastor and only the church can legitimately dismiss the pastor. I'm not encouraging pastors to force a showdown in business meeting. I simply want pastors to remember this fact. You are the God-called pastor of your church until you, or the church, decide otherwise. Don't sell yourself short. Too often, pastors give up and throw in the towel early. Remember, "hard" is a long way from "can't do it anymore."

I am not only concerned for pastors. I'm also concerned for churches. Forced resignations or dismissals are devastating to pastors, pastor's families and churches. It takes pastors and their families *years* to work through the pain of a forced termination. It takes churches *generations* to do so.

Don't resign. Not until it is time. But if you decide the pressure is significant enough and you don't want to force a showdown at business meeting, here is what you do.

Do not just suddenly resign. *The moment you resign you lose all power and influence.* You empower those who stand against you and you undercut your friends and supporters. Before you resign, negotiate a fair severance package and work out an appropriate timetable to leave. Make certain you receive compensation that is fair and will take care of your family for a legitimate length of time. The severance package *must be in writing*. If church leaders refuse to negotiate a severance before you resign, then *don't resign*. Don't forget, *the church called you and only the church has the right to dismiss you*. Again, once you resign you lose all power and influence.

A fair severance is not only good for the pastor and his family; it is good for the church. On several occasions, I've witnessed churches be generous with their pastor when he left the church under difficult circumstances. Inevitably that generosity helped the church heal more quickly. The pastor's friends and supporters felt the church at least tried to act fairly. The pastor's detractors felt the church made an effort to be Christian in the midst of tragic circumstances.

What's A Pastor to Do?

Pastors are never victims. We are children of the King. We are called and empowered to serve the Master. There are always wise decisions to be made under any circumstance. As we focus on the Lord and walk by faith, He will empower us to live His perfect will. We will thrive as His servants fulfilling His divine call.

Chapter Seven

LEADERSHIP

Pastor, are you a leader? That is like asking a father if he leads his family, a teacher if she leads her class or a business owner if she leads her business. Fathers, teachers and business owners are leaders by virtue of their position. Every pastor is a leader. Regardless of the level of giftedness he has in staff management, vision casting or organizational systems, he is a leader. By virtue of his calling and position, the pastor is to lead his church.

Lead with Your Life (*Being*)

The title and theme of this book is *The Key Is To Be*. You must *be someone* before you can *do something*. Effective *doing* comes from effective *being*. The most powerful leadership technique a pastor has is his own life.

Jesus said, *"I have set you an example that you should do as I have done for you."* Paul wrote, *"Follow my example, as I follow the example of Christ."* We must always remember that the pastor's highest calling is to model the Christian life. It is not to preach, grow the church or even win the lost, but to live for Christ. To live in a way that models Christ. We will have the greatest impact for God by how we live our lives. *The key is to be*!

Pastor, as you love your people, they will grow to love each other. As you live an honest, responsible and generous life, your people will learn and follow. As you serve your wife with respect and care, your men will honor and cherish their wives. As you and your wife rear your children to love God, parents in your church will do the same with theirs. As you manage your personal finances wisely, church members will follow your example. As you walk closely with the Lord, those in your congregation will grow in their walk with God.

In 1931 Mother Teresa went to Calcutta, India to teach at St. Mary's High School. She was so moved by the plight of the poor that in 1948 she received permission to leave the school and begin a ministry among the poorest of the poor in the slums of Calcutta. One of her primary objectives was to bring a little comfort to people who were alone and dying on the streets of that massive city. Little did she know that her example would attract nuns from all over the world to serve at her side. She never dreamed she would be internationally known and receive world-wide acclaim. Mother Teresa believed we were not created to be successful, but to be obedient to God. On several occasions she observed, "I am a little pencil in the hand of a writing God who is sending a love letter to the world." Mother Teresa's power was in her life. It came from who she was. Her effectiveness and leadership came from her example.

Lead by Doing

Many pastors are frustrated by the lack of energy and ministry activity in their church. Pastors long to see their churches more involved in outreach and evangelism, but church members are apathetic. Pastors ache to see their churches more active in missions both locally and globally, but their people aren't motivated.

What's a pastor to do? Some pastors excuse their church's behavior by believing this is simply the culture of the modern church and there is nothing we can do about it. They explain that the church is stuck on an internal (selfish) focus and pastors are powerless to change it. Is that true? It *is* true that most churches are internally focused. It is *not* true that pastors are powerless to do anything about it. There are many things we can do.

Gandhi said, "Be the change you want to see in the world." Pastor, even if your church won't actively participate in an outreach ministry, no one can keep you from visiting the lost. Even if your church isn't supportive of a missions ministry, no one can keep you from personally getting involved in a local missions effort or going on a mission trip. As a pastor, you lead by living your call to ministry and God's call to your church. Your example has more power than any committee decision (or failure to decide) or any business meeting vote (or failure to vote). Your church may formally decide not to enact an outreach program or be actively involved in missions, but no one can keep you from obeying God's call.

As I write this book, Phil and Nelta St. Laurent, pastor and wife at little Bois D'Arc Baptist Church, are in India on a mission trip. They are working with Pastor Nazir and Pastor Gulzar to share the Gospel with people who have never heard of the grace of Jesus. By modeling international missions, Phil is raising the missions temperature and missions participation of his church. He is leading by *doing*.

I was pastor of a wonderful church near downtown Kansas City, Missouri. The church was an older congregation that had become internally focused. We tried several things to move the church to a more evangelistic and missions mindset. Nothing worked. I was frustrated and discouraged. I fervently prayed the Lord would change the church. Most of my time and energy was spent caring for church members and maintaining the machinery of the church.

One deacon in the church had a strong heart for evangelism. With my encouragement, he went to a neighboring church and received Evangelism Explosion training. I served as his prayer partner while he took the training. Once he completed the training, we decided we needed to be nationally certified so we could implement Evangelism Explosion in our church. By this time, I realized the lack of evangelism and missions in our church was my fault. How could I expect my people to do missions and faithfully witness if I wasn't doing it myself? The deacon and I went to Ft.

Lauderdale, Florida, received training at Coral Ridge Presbyterian Church and implemented Evangelism Explosion in our church.

Our first semester we had a grand total of four in Evangelism Explosion. Over the next few years, the ministry grew to average fifteen to twenty each semester. During those years, we trained scores of people to share their faith and saw many come to Christ. We also witnessed the spirit in the church move from being internally focused to a focus on missions and evangelism.

Pastors are never powerless to lead their churches forward. We always have the power of our life and service at our disposal.

Vision

Leadership means vision. We must have vision if we are to lead our own lives as well as lead others. Vision may be something as grandiose as constructing a new sanctuary or as simple as teaching a child to read. Parents must have a vision for their children if they want their children to reach their potential. A builder must have a design in mind and plans in hand before he can build a house. A coach must have organizational structure and plays worked out to effectively coach her team. A Sunday School teacher must have the lesson planned and a teaching method in mind to successfully teach his class. A pastor must have a vision (however big or small) of where he wants his church to go if he has any hope of leading his church forward.

A pastor's vision begins with God. We are familiar with the King James Version of Proverbs 29:18, *"Where there is no vision, the people perish: but he that keepeth the law, happy is he."* We need to remember this verse is not speaking about a general vision or some man-induced vision. It is speaking of a vision from God. The NIV translates it like this, *"Where there is no revelation, the people cast off restraint; but blessed is he who keeps the law."*

Pastor, your vision for your church comes from God. If you don't have vision for your church or if your vision is weak or fuzzy, it's time to spend time with the Lord. Never doubt whether or not God has a vision for you and your church. He does. Never wonder whether or not God will reveal His vision to you. He will.

I love the way The Message translates the verse, *"If people can't see what God is doing, they stumble all over themselves; But when they attend to what he reveals, they are most blessed."*

Stay in touch with God and He will reveal His vision to you. Once you've captured that vision, proceed with confidence. The Lord will give you the resources, energy and help to achieve it.

One of the exciting parts of my job as Director of the Association is hearing pastors share their God-revealed vision and then watching that vision become reality.

Vaughn Weatherford (National Heights) had a dream of adding a new worship service to the Sunday morning schedule at National Heights. The purpose was to reach young families. That dream is now reality.

Ty Harmon (Galloway) had a vision of adding needed ministerial staff at Galloway. Today Ty is blessed to have additional staff assisting him in leading Galloway to new heights.

Many years ago Boone Middleton (Golden Avenue) had a dream of involving his church in world missions. He preached on missions, modeled missions, and provided opportunities for hands-on missions experiences. Through Boone's vision and leadership, Golden Avenue has a strong missions heart that expresses itself in world-wide missions involvement.

John's Vision

John Marshall (Second Baptist) begins his book, *Through The Eyes Of God,* with a challenging story.

Years ago my family received free tickets to a St. Louis Cardinals' baseball game. Upon entering Busch Stadium, ushers kept motioning us higher and higher up stairways, and farther and farther around the building.

Finally, we arrived at our seats in dead center field, in the section farthest from home plate. We were so far away from the batter that we would see him swing at the ball, and then later hear the sound of the bat hitting it. We were too far away to see the ball's movement off the bat, and had to watch for running fielders to tell where the ball had headed. We were on the outskirts of the action, barely involved. The game was distant reality, something way off in the distance. That's how I felt a few years ago when the Lord began to burden my heart for worldwide missions. I felt as if I were way off in the bleachers somewhere. I could hear Jesus giving the Great Commission, but it seemed only a faint whisper, a barely audible echo. I was in the stadium, but the game was not a vital factor in my life.

God used that experience and vision to motivate John to get in the game of world missions. Through John's vision, Second Baptist has become a national leader in missions, sending thousands to the field to serve and giving millions of dollars for missions causes. John concludes his book by declaring, "Ruth, our church and I are no longer on the sidelines. We're now in the middle of the action, on the cutting edge of the Great Commission."

It began with a vision.

Faith

Against seemingly insurmountable odds, Moses led by faith when he brought the Israelites out of Egypt and across the Red Sea. With fear, doubt and failure, David led by faith as he led Israel to conquer their enemies and establish a strong nation. Nehemiah stood alone as he led by faith and inspired God's people to rebuild the wall around Jerusalem and thereby rebuild the nation. Barnabas led by faith when he befriended new Christian Paul. Peter led by faith when he went against tradition and visited the home of

Cornelius. Jesus led by faith when He told some fishermen to, *"Come, follow me"* as well as when He breathed His last and said, *"It is finished."*

Pastor, when was the last step of faith you took in your personal life? When was the last step of faith you led your church to take? Hebrews 11 states, *"And without faith it is impossible to please God..."* If we want our lives and ministries to please God, we must *live* and *lead* by faith.

What is the next step of faith your church needs to take? Does your church need to be more intentional about ministering in your neighborhood? What about involvement in a missions effort locally or globally? Perhaps your church needs to plant a new church or begin a ministry in an apartment complex. Maybe you need to simply address the barriers that keep your church from moving forward.

As pastor, your church will not advance until you lead them. You have to step out of the boat, walk on water for a few steps and then invite people to join you. If you don't, your church will remain in the boat and remain secure (or not secure) in its own little world.

My greatest fear is standing before the Lord and hearing, "Mike, if you had only trusted me and lived by faith, I had so much more for you. If you had only led your Association by faith, I had so much more for your Association. Here, let me show you all you missed because you didn't *live* and *lead* by faith." Yikes! That's scary to think about.

When I first met Winston Barnett (LifeBuilders) he was ministering in one apartment complex on the North side of Springfield. He had a handful of people serving with him. I've watched Winston and LifeBuilders take step after step of faith. Oftentimes, his steps of faith appeared to be nothing more than wishful imagination. As I write this book, Winston is ministering in five apartment complexes around Springfield with nearly fifty people and several churches serving with him.

In 1999 Jess Roberds (Golden Harvest) came to visit me. He told me about his dream to start a new church. Jess had successfully pastored several churches in the Association. His most recent pastorate involved relocation and construction of a brand new church facility. Now Jess was considering starting from scratch and planting a new church. As Jess shared his vision with me, I thought to myself, "Jess, you and Charlotte aren't as young as you used to be. Are you sure you want to take on a project like this? This is the type of thing young guys do (and many of them fail)." I promised Jess my support and prayers, but I honestly wondered if he could do it. Now we know the rest of the story. Through faith and hard work, Jess and Charlotte established Golden Harvest on the west side of town. It is a thriving congregation ministering in its community and seeing many come to Christ.

Pastor, what's next for you and your church? Refuse to get comfortable. Comfort leads to complacency. Don't let the naysayers stifle the Spirit and cut off your leadership. God is pleased when we take bold steps of faith.

A church I pastored was in the early stages of a financial campaign. The purpose of the campaign was to raise money for a major building project. Several people were opposed to what we were doing and the direction the church was headed. The financial campaign was chaired by a feisty old retired railroad man. At the kick-off of the campaign, he got up before the church and said, "Folks, this train is leaving the station. We want everyone to come with us. If you're with us, hop on for a great ride. If not, we will wave "goodbye" and leave you standing at the station."

Faith Is The Victory

We are challenged and inspired by the great John Yates and Ira Sankey Hymn, *Faith Is The Victory*. The first verse and chorus are a call to arms!

Encamped along the hills of light,
Ye Christian soldiers, rise
And press the battle ere the night
Shall veil the glowing skies.

Against the foe in vales below
Let all our strength be hurled;
Faith is the victory we know,
That overcomes the world.

Faith is the victory! Faith is the Victory!
Oh, glorious victory that overcomes the world.

With faith, a pastor will lead his church to glorious and eternal victory.

CONCLUSION

One time an angry church member came storming into my office, sat down, looked across the desk at me and said, "I hate you."

Another time I baptized a man and when he came up out of the water he raised his hands, yelled "**yes**," and the congregation burst into applause.

The pastorate is both exhilarating and excruciating. It is energizing, fun, sad, lonely and will drain you of every ounce of life. It is the toughest calling and the most rewarding work on the earth.

The Key Is To Be. Remember this truth: *People, circumstances and your own limitations may keep you from **doing** something you want to do, but no one or nothing can keep you from **being** who God wants you to be.*

May our lives and ministries *be* exceptional as we live for His glory and Kingdom expansion!

SOURCES

Chapter 1: The Key Is To Be

2. *"The Lord God"*: Genesis 2:7.
5. *"Moses said"*: Exodus 3:13-14.
5. *"We do not"*: II Corinthians 10:12.
6. Bill Russell, *Eulogy of Wilt Chamberlain.* Time Magazine, October 25, 1999.
6. *"Martha was distracted"*: Luke 10:40-42.
6. Robert Dale, *To Dream Again.* Nashville: Broadman Press, 1981, pg. 90.
7. Shakespeare:William Shakespeare, *Hamlet*, Act III.
7. *"It's in Christ"*: Ephesians 1:11. *The Message.*
8. Plato: quoted in *The Ten Golden Rules* by M. A. Soupios and Panos Mourdoukoutas, Charlottesville, VA.: Hampton Roads Publishing Company, Inc., 2009, Scene 1, p.1.
8. Blackaby: *Experiencing God*, Henry Blackaby and Claude King. Nashville. LifeWay Press, 1990, p. 18.
11. Abraham Lincoln, *The Wit and Wisdom of Abraham Lincoln* by Abraham Lincoln and Bob Blaisdell. Edited by Alex Ayres. New York: Penguin Group, 1992, P.12.
12. J. R. R. Tolkien, *The Hobbit.* New York: Ballantine Books, 1982, introduction.

Chapter 2: Your Church's Top Priority

17. *"The Whole Town"*: Mark 1:33.
17. Major W. Ian Thomas, *The Saving Life of Christ.* Grand Rapids: Zondervan Publishing House, 1961, p. 63.
17. *"Got up"*: Mark 1:35.
17. *"Immediately Jesus"*: Mark 6:45.

19. E. Stanley Jones: Quoted in Gordon Mcdonald, *Ordering Your Private World.* Nashville: Thomas Nelson Publishers, 2003, p. 149.
19. *"Remain in me"*: John 15:4.
21. *"Work out your"*: Philippians 2:12.
21. *"Love the Lord"*: Matthew 22:37-38.
22. Gary Thomas, *Sacred Pathways.* Grand Rapids: Zondervan Publishing House, 1996.
23. *"Moses then wrote"*: Exodus 24:4.
24. Gary Thomas, *Seeking the Face of God.* Eugene: Harvest House Publishers, 1994, p.105.

Chapter 3: Cherish Your Family

28. *"Here is a trustworthy"*: I Timothy 3:1-5.
29. *"Love your wives"*: Ephesians 5:25-28, 31.
33. *"Remember the Sabbath"*: Exodus 20:8-10.
33. *"The Sabbath"*: Mark 2:27.
34. *"Fathers, do not exasperate"*: Ephesians 6:4.
34. *"Fathers, don't exasperate"*: Ephesians 6:4. *The Message.*
36. *"Fathers, don't exasperate"*: Ibid.
37. Philip Yancey, *What's So Amazing About Grace.* Grand Rapids: Zondervan Publishing House, 1997.
38. Father and Paco: Ibid., p.37-38.
38. *"Take them by"*: Ephesians 6:4. *The Message*

Chapter 4: Don't Waste Pain

41. *"Consider it pure joy"*: James 1:2-4, 12.
41. *"My Brothers"*: James 1:2.
42. *"The Spirit himself"*: Romans 8:16-17.
44. *"Whenever you face"*: James 1:2.
45. *"Shake the dust"*: Matthew 10:14.
46. Paul Brand and Philip Yancey, *The Gift of Pain.* Grand Rapids: Zondervan Publishing House, 1993.
47. Story of rats: Ibid p. 127.

47. *"Consider it pure"*: James 1:2.
47. *"Rejoice in our"*: Romans 5:3.
47. *"Our trials will"*: I Peter 1:7.
47. *"Blessed are you"*: Matthew 5:11-12.
48. Benjamin Franklin: quoted in John Maxwell, *Failing Forward.* Nashville: Thomas Nelson, Inc. 2000, p.137.
48. *"Refiner's fire"*: Malachi 3:2-3.
48. Madam Guyon: quoted in *Finding Peace* by Paula Peisner Cox, Naperville, Illinois: Sourcebooks, Inc., 2004, p.151.
48. *"Thorn in the flesh"*: II Corinthians 12:7.
48. John Maxwell, *Failing Forward.* Nashville: Thomas Nelson, Inc., 2000, p. 137.
52. Robert Browning Hamilton, *Along the Road.* Nashville: Abingdon Press, 1995, p. 12.
52. C.S. Lewis: quoted in *Lewis Agonistes* by Louis Markos, Nashville: Broadman and Holman, 2003, p.104.
53. Abbot John the Dwarf: quoted in *The Wisdom of the Desert* by Thomas Merton, New York: New Directions Publishing Corporation, 1970, p. 57.
53. *"My grace is sufficient"*: II Corinthians 12:9.

Chapter 5: Balance

56. Robert Louis Stephenson: quoted in *The Executive's Book of Quotations* by Julia Vitullo-Martin and J. Robert Moskin, New York: Oxford University Press, 1994, p.41.
56. John Ortberg, *Overcoming Your Shadow Mission.* Grand Rapids: Zondervan, 2008, p. 9.
56. *"For the Son"*: Luke 19:10.
59. Mark Buchanan, *The Rest of God.* Nashville: W Publishing Group, 2006, p. 1.
59. Gordon MacDonald, *Ordering Your Private World.* Nashville: Thomas Nelson Publishers, 2003, p. 32.
59. *"Six Days"*: Exodus 20:9-10.
60. Richard Swenson, *Margin.* Colorado Springs: NavPress, 1992, p. 13.

60. Story of moon and paper: Ibid., p. 45
61. "margin…is having breath": Ibid., pp. 111-119.
62. Stephen R. Covey, A. Roger Merrill and Rebecca R. Merrill, *First Things First*. New York: Simon & Schuster,1996, p.88.
63. Abraham Lincoln: quoted in *The Little, Brown Book of Anecdotes* edited by Clifton Fadiman. Boston: Little, Brown and Company, 1985, p. 359.
63. *The Goose and The Golden Eggs: Aesop's Fables*. New York: Lancer Books, Inc., 1968, p. 28.

Chapter 6: What's A Pastor To Do?

66. Stephen R. Covey, *The 7 Habits of Highly Effective People*. New York: Simon & Schuster, 1989, p. 287.
68. Frank Schaeffer, *Crazy For God*. Cambridge: Carroll and Graf Publishers, 2007.
69. Eric Hoffer: quoted in *The Science of Success* by James Arthur Ray. Carlsbad, CA: Sun Ark Press, 2003, p. 27.
70. *"The Word became"*: John 1:14 & 16.
71. Haldor Lillenas, *Wonderful Grace of Jesus*. The Baptist Hymnal, Nashville: Convention Press, 1991, p. 328.
72. *Developing a Christian Mean Streak*, article by Stephen Brown. Christianity Today Leadership Library.com, *Leadership,* Spring 1987.
73. *"You must be"*: John 3:7.
73. *"If your brother"*: Matthew 18:15.
73. Jimmy Draper at Glorieta in the Ozarks Leadership Conference, September, 2007.
79. George Washington: quoted in *The American Spirit: Meeting the Challenges of September 11* by Editors of One Nation and George W. Bush. Edited by Robert Sullivan. New York: Life Books, 2001. p.159.
79. *"Father, if you"*: Luke 22:42.
79. *"Yet not my"*: Luke 22:42.

Chapter 7: Leadership

87. *"I have set"*: John 13:15.
87. *"Follow my example"*: I Corinthians 11:1.
88. Mother Teresa: quoted in *Mother Teresa's Secret Fire* by Joseph Langford. Huntington, IN: Our Sunday Visitor Publishing Division, 2008, p. 48.
89. Ghandi: quoted in *Welcome to the Wisdom of the World* by Joan Chittister. Grand Rapids: Eerdmans Publishing Co., 2007, p.147.
91. John Marshall, *Through the Eyes of God.* Nashville: Randall House Publications, 2005, pp. 1-2.
92. Ibid., p. 118.
93. *"Come, follow me"*: Matthew 4:19.
93. *"It is finished"*: John 19:30
93. *"And without faith"*: Hebrews 11:6.
94. John H. Yates and Ira D. Sankey, *Faith Is The Victory.* The Baptist Hymnal, Nashville: Convention Press, 1991, p. 413.